MIDLAND RED NORTH

by

Neil MacDonald

ISBN 1 898432 26 0

Front Cover Illustration

A gleaming 1711 (WHP 121 Y) pauses at Milford Common to pick up a passenger. This was one of the first series in the rebodying programme where former London and Country Leyland Tigers were given a new lease of life by East Lancashire Coachbuilders.

Photo: Neil MacDonald

Produced in the United Kingdom

MIDLAND RED NORTH

by

Neil MacDonald

Contents

Foreword

Having spent almost thirty years in the bus industry I must admit to having become a little bit of an enthusiast for the product which has looked after me well since my early days as a bus conductor with the City of Oxford Motor Services Limited. Hence the opportunity to assist, in a small way, in providing information for this excellent book was seized upon immediately.

My first association with the old Midland Red company took the form of running joint bus services from Oxford to Birmingham, Coventry and Stratford-upon-Avon. I recall vividly the bi-annual meetings which would take place at popular 'watering holes' to allow the respective management teams to discuss matters of mutual interest, which just occasionally included the joint services!

My other association with the company was the annual cricket match in the Skyrme Cup competition; my recollections are that over the years the honours were even, but I doubt that John Hargreaves would see it that way.

Connection with the affairs of Midland Red ceased for me in 1986 and was not to surface again until 10 September 1990 when I was appointed Managing Director of the Bee Line Buzz Company in Manchester, under the Drawlane Transport Group banner.

The Managing Director of Midland Red North was then Chris Hilditch and I became quite familiar with his company, which was also part of the Group, and I must say it was in much better condition than my operation. How I envied Chris the opportunity to run what was obviously a company with a long, proud history and whose operating territory covered such a vastly contrasting area. Unlike me, who could leave my Hulme Hall Road base in Manchester and still be driving through built-up area for miles down the road, Chris could choose his menu for the day, which could well be Oswestry for breakfast, Crewe for lunch and Stafford for tea.

Imagine my delight at being given the opportunity to take over as Managing Director of Midland Red North on 12 October 1992, a post which I held until 1 August 1994 when I was appointed Executive Chairman of the Midlands Division of British Bus plc; thankfully my duties still cover MRN.

During the past two years a great deal of investment has gone into the company and is set to continue over the next five years. I hope that the new livery is pleasing to our customers and to those who cast an 'enthusiastic' eye over the fleet. I like to think that it can be associated with the image of a truly remarkable company with a long history of providing public transport services.

Turning now to the author of this magnificent book, I would like to give my sincere thanks to Neil MacDonald for affording us the privilege of contributing towards some of the facts and figures contained within it. Neil has an amazing eye for detail and his book gives a real flavour of how Midland Red has changed over the years.

I would also wish to thank Colin Chattoe and his colleagues for their tireless efforts in supplying information which has assisted Neil in preparing this book and to all members of the staff of Midland Red North who continue to make it a company with which I am truly proud to be associated.

Richard C Bowler
January 1995

Preface

Having lived in Staffordshire for some 27 years I have come to regard Midland Red as a necessary part of local life. I have watched the company change from the giant organisation which filled the West Midlands with its presence, through the enforced split into the so-called 'compass point' companies in 1973 and on to individually owned subsidiaries of three of the major bus-owning groups of today. It has given me no small pleasure to watch the resurgence of some of the image of the past with the adoption by Midland Red North of a livery which has more than a passing relationship to that of the Birmingham and Midland Motor Omnibus Company.

Every author of a historical subject tries to strike a balance between an assembly of factual information and anecdotal commentary. In this endeavour I have taken the liberty, on occasions, of introducing interpretations and opinions which are my own and which do not necessarily reflect any official views. It is my hope that these signs of gentle bias and prejudice which are always part of the make-up of the serious student of transport matters will be forgiven, should they conflict with the reader's own perceptions.

In writing this work I have had much help and co-operation from many sources and individuals. My thanks are due to all of them but special mention must be made of the support from Richard Bowler (now Executive Chairman) who was instrumental in allowing the project to start, and from Colin Chattoe and his colleagues at MidlandRed North headquarters; in particular I am grateful for the help of Alan Gaze who has provided a mass of information on the numerous changes to the fleet. With the passage of time many queries were presented to all of them and, in spite of the distraction from their primary function of running a bus company, answers were found.

At the garages staff at all levels have been co-operative in the extreme. It has been a pleasant experience for me to find that the genuine interest of the true busman still survives even in these times when cynicism and disdain are so apparent in our society. It is not possible to name all who have contributed to this work but I hope that the finished article will bring to each of them its own form of recognition.

It is necessary, however, to mention the Rev. Geoffrey Smith (Haughton), Gordon Weston and colleagues (Stafford) and Charles Roberts (Liverpool) who have allowed me to borrow from their photographic collections. Midland Red North itself provided much additional material to complement my own collection and again this is much appreciated.

On the factual side, apart from MRN's input, I am greatly indebted to John Birks who was kind enough to guide me to much useful information regarding the background to those earlier events which culminated in the splitting of Midland Red Omnibus Company into the six smaller companies, and to Ian Mitchell for allowing me to access his personal records of the events in the run-up to privatisation. Fred Taylor, Financial Director at that time, has also made a valuable contribution to my understanding of the financial situation faced by the Management Buy-Out Team.

The chapter on fleet development includes several tables the contents of which are based upon data provided by the PSV Circle, in its Fleet History PD19 and subsequent monthly news sheets; the facility to use this information is gratefully acknowledged. In that same chapter much additional information has been provided by Alan Gaze.

Sources of photographic material are acknowledged where known, other than those items provided by the author or from MRN's own archive. Should there be any omissions in this respect the author and publishers apologise for the inadvertent oversight.

I have had much assistance from David Meredith and other colleagues at Venture Publications and my sincere thanks are due to them.

Finally I thank my dear wife Anna. She has encouraged me and has quietly put up with many months where much of our home has been taken over by Midland Red North in the shape of photographs, timetables and other documents.

Walton-on-the-Hill
Stafford

January 1995

A summer's day sees a smart 12 metre Tiger 1728 (B 108 KPF) steadily climbing towards Satnall Hills on the A513 Stafford-Lichfield road across Cannock Chase. Its 'dayglo' destination display proclaims that it is on a school holiday extension of the 825 service beyond Tamworth to Drayton Manor Park.

Chapter 1

Setting the Scene

The Birmingham and Midland Motor Omnibus Company, destined to be known universally as 'Midland Red', was incorporated in 1904. Its early history has been told in fine detail elsewhere[1] and the reader is referred to that excellent treatment of a fascinating story. The end of that story is effectively dated as 14 March 1968, the day when the Midland Red company became a wholly owned subsidiary of the Transport Holding Company, the organisation set up under the 1962 Transport Act to manage nationalised omnibus undertakings. Midland Red had been a subsidiary of the British Electric Traction Company whose violent opposition to the concept of nationalisation was well publicised in the 1950s and 1960s but which came in the end to an accommodation with the negotiators of the THC for the sale of all its UK bus interests. There seems little doubt that the deteriorating state of the bus industry, with falling revenue and increased operating costs, was a decisive factor in the about turn of BET's attitude; pressure from the then Minister of Transport, Barbara Castle, also played a significant part in persuading BET to turn away from its well-stated opposition to nationalisation of its bus assets[2].

The 1968 Transport Act then had its effect. The Transport Holding Company was wound up and the combined Tilling and BET bus fleets were transferred to the ownership of the new National Bus Company, the change taking place on 1 January 1969. There was a second consequence of the 1968 Act. Midland Red had for many years developed and built its own buses, in several respects demonstrating innovative features which influenced other builders. The contributions of L G Wyndham Shire and his successor Donald M Sinclair as Chief Engineers will remain as milestones in the history of British bus engineering. Unfortunately those same financial difficulties which had affected the operating side of the company were also casting a cloud over the design and construction activities at Carlyle Road Works, Birmingham and it was thus no surprise when it was announced shortly after integration within NBC that design work would cease and that production would be run down. The last vehicle built to BMMO design, an S23 single-decker fleet number 5991, left the Carlyle Road Works on 5 January 1970.

The main reason for the demise of Carlyle Road was, however, a political one. NBC, which had inherited the bus and coach building operations of Bristol Commercial Vehicles and Eastern Coach Works, announced in July 1969 the creation of a joint venture with British Leyland Motor Corporation to build a new bus of revolutionary integral design and it was clear that this decision would have a profound effect on vehicle acquisition policy for NBC operating companies. That story has been well told by Doug Jack[3].

There is another aspect of the 1968 Transport Act which concerns this story. Under the terms of the Act, one of whose aims was to introduce facilities for improvement of public transport co-ordination and planning in the major conurbations, Public Transport Authorities (PTAs) were established. The PTAs in turn were to have executive agencies, Public Transport Executives (PTEs), under their control whose function was to apply direct managerial influence upon the operating organisations within the defined area. PTAs were to be established according to the original list on Merseyside, in the sprawling conurbation around Manchester (SELNEC), in the West Midlands, and on Tyneside; subsequently PTAs were also formed in West Yorkshire and South Yorkshire whilst the Tyneside one was expanded to include Wearside. In Scotland a PTE was created somewhat later by the new Strathclyde Regional Council for Greater Glasgow. In the case of West Midlands the defined area included parts of south Staffordshire and north Warwickshire in addition to the County Boroughs of the City of Birmingham, West Bromwich, Walsall, Wolverhampton, Smethwick and Solihull.

Amongst the powers given to these new authorities was that of acquiring the assets of local authority transport undertakings within the defined areas and this was done as soon as the Act was passed. Thus within the West Midlands the undertakings owned by Birmingham, West Bromwich,

An example of a BMMO D9 is preserved at Wythall. 5339 spent its last days in service based at Stafford. Subsequently it was retained for preservation by Midland Red Omnibus Company and was on loan to MRN for two years from 1982 until 1984.

Walsall, and Wolverhampton Corporations were brought under the ownership of West Midlands PTE on 1 October 1969. Following upon the local government reorganisation of 1974, when West Midlands Metropolitan County was established and the area of the PTA was modified to become identical with the new metropolitan county, the undertaking owned by the City of Coventry was integrated within the PTE. This re-drawing of the PTA area also meant that those parts of adjoining counties which had been within the original PTA area were now 'freed'.

The 1968 Act also made provision for the PTAs to acquire the businesses of other operators within the defined territories, where they regarded it as essential to their co-ordination and planning strategies. In the event the West Midlands PTA sought to apply this provision as did the SELNEC authority which took over the operations owned by the Lancashire United Transport Company and those of the North Western Road Car Company within its designated area in 1969; following the 1974 changes to local authorities SELNEC became the Greater Manchester PTA. In Tyne and Wear and West Yorkshire the PTAs required the major bus operators outside PTE ownership to adopt the PTE livery for operations within the PTA boundaries, thus avoiding acquisition of assets of those operators.

West Midlands PTA had earlier taken the view that because of the extensive network of urban bus services operated by Midland Red in the Black Country, its traditional core of activity, effective transport planning and co-ordination would only be possible if the services and rolling stock were under direct ownership of the PTE. On this basis, therefore, negotiations were opened with National Bus Company, by now the owners of the former BET-owned Midland Red, leading to the purchase of all assets connected with the Midland Red operations in the Black Country area of what was to become West Midlands Metropolitan County. Agreement was reached on 27 June 1973 and the actual transfer of assets was executed on 3 December of the same year. The Midland Red garages at Sheepcote Street (Birmingham), Oldbury, Stourbridge, Hartshill, Dudley and Sutton Coldfield passed to the PTE[4].

At the same time changes were made to certain services which straddled the boundary of the PTA area. For example, the long 65/865 route from Dudley to Stafford, worked jointly by Midland Red and Walsall Corporation was split such that the Dudley-Walsall section became exclusively a WMPTE operation whilst the remainder of the route, still numbered 865, from Walsall to Stafford was now solely a Midland Red service. In return Midland Red received a number of ex-Wolverhampton Corporation services, such as those to Bridgnorth, Brewood and Cannock; initially these services were operated by Midland Red from its Cradley Heath garage, to be transferred to a new Cannock garage in Delta Way in February 1977. Ex-Walsall Corporation routes in the Cannock area to Hednesford, Rawnsley and Lichfield were not involved and continued as WMPTE operations from Walsall garage; perhaps WMPTE felt that they had given enough. One other consequence of this extensive restructuring of Midland Red was the passing of the time honoured Birmingham and

Midland Motor Omnibus Company name; on 29 March 1974, perhaps to recognise that times had indeed changed, the company was re-registered simply as the Midland Red Omnibus Company Limited. Birmingham (and the Black Country) had ceased to be the focus of the company's activities.

Without operations in the Black Country Midland Red became a difficult organisation to manage, being described somewhat whimsically as the company 'with the hole in the middle', an allusion to then current advertising for a well-known mint confection. It happened that National Bus Company had been considering a restructuring of Midland Red prior to the events described above. It had been concerned that in the changing market conditions, which involved *inter alia* seeking subsidy support for many rural services from local authorities, the large structure of the Midland Red company was becoming inappropriate[5]. One idea canvassed was for the company to be dismembered and the parts passed to the control of neighbouring NBC subsidiaries, *viz.* PMT, Crosville, Red and White, Bristol Omnibus Company, City of Oxford, United Counties and Trent[5a]; a later alternative, which avoided the political and practical problems of the first idea, was that Midland Red be divided into four autonomous operating companies. The events of 1973 in the West Midlands certainly gave impetus to further thinking on these proposals and eventually the latter course of action was decided upon.

1976 had seen an exercise which would have great significance not only for Midland Red but eventually for the whole of the bus industry outside London. Midland Red commissioned a joint programme in conjunction with NBC Consultancy Services and the independent consultants Colin Buchanan and Partners with the objective of identifying in given areas service structures which could be maintained with commercially acceptable fares. This study, named the Viable Network Project (VNP), was successfully applied in the areas based on Stratford-upon-Avon, Evesham and Kidderminster during 1977. VNP was then developed further to provide a scheme which could be applied across the whole of National Bus Company and was introduced as the Market Analysis Project (MAP). MAP achieved such success with NBC that it was adopted in essentially the same form by the Scottish Bus Group under the banner SCOTMAP and ultimately was to influence many local authority bus operations.

In summary MAP brought radical change to bus services and route networks throughout the country by focusing upon the needs of the market and identifying optimum utilisation of vehicles. Route networks which had developed, like Topsy, over many decades were drastically modified or even abandoned to be replaced with ones which were constructed from computer analysis of the extensive data gathered from passenger journey surveys, vehicle mileage figures and revenue earned. A more detailed treatment of MAP and its results is available elsewhere[5b].

Midland Red, having been the pioneer in the creation of VNP, then applied MAP throughout its territory. For the sector which would become Midland Red North MAP schemes were put in train in the Cannock, Stafford,

Tamworth, Telford, Wellington and Shrewsbury areas.

Until 1977 town services in Telford and the many communities which had been brought together to form the new town concept had been provided by a number of independent operators, several of whom had a single route. The situation clearly concerned the Development Corporation and discussions were opened involving also Shropshire County Council, Midland Red and the independents. The outcome was that a formula was found by which the seven independents, listed below, sold their stage carriage interests to Midland Red who were then charged by the two local authorities with the task of recasting the service network in the Telford New Town area.

Independent Operators in Telford/Wellington acquired by Midland Red

Ashley and Sons	G Cooper and Sons, Oakengates*
H Brown	Priory Motors
F Lowe	G Smith
T Hoggins and Sons, Wrockwardine Wood*	

*Only four vehicles came with these businesses, two Bedford YRQ/Duple vehicles from Coopers and two Seddon Pennine VIs with Plaxton bodies from Hoggins. Numbered 2146, 2147 and 2149, 2150 respectively by Midland Red; all four had gone by the time MRN was formed.

The recast network was introduced on 1 April 1978 with a zonal fare structure. The MAP-inspired restructuring, in the then fashionable marketing vein, was presented under the branding 'Tellus', unkindly thought to have been a misprint for 'Telbus''.

Tamworth area was next to see the results of an MAP survey and the re-organised services there were introduced with the identity 'Mercian' on 1 September 1979. Stafford and Cannock followed with the introduction of revised services and the name 'Chaserider' on 31 May 1980. Finally Shrewsbury town services together with country routes operated from Shrewsbury, Wellington and Ludlow garages were given the MAP treatment and the resulting changes took effect on 24 November 1980 using the 'Hotspur' identity.

In common with practice in other NBC companies these local identities were applied to buses as well as bus stops, timetables and promotional material. At first the new names were added to the white band at cantrail level alongside the 'Midland Red' and the National 'double N' logo. On double-deck buses this information also appeared at cantrail level.

The revenue of Midland Red had suffered significantly following the loss of the lucrative Black Country urban services. Despite cost reductions involving both staff and vehicles the situation had deteriorated to such an extent by 1980 that an operating shortfall of some £5 million was forecast for the 1981-2 financial year; with financial support of £2.3 million it was clear that drastic action was necessary and plans for the break-up of Midland Red were put into action.

At midnight on Saturday 5 September 1981 the company was split into six units comprising four bus companies, a coach company and a company named Midland Red Omnibus Company Ltd which was to inherit the Carlyle Works as well as being a property holding company. The four bus companies were named, with due lack of imagination, Midland Red (East), Midland Red (South), Midland Red (West) and Midland Red (North). The registered offices and company secretarial functions were placed with the NBC subsidiaries adjacent to the territories of the new entities. In the case of Midland Red (North) the registered office was at Woodhouse Street, Stoke-on-Trent, the headquarters of Potteries Motor Traction Company. (It is interesting to conjecture whether the name of the off-the-shelf company used in the case of MRN, Calm Image Limited, might not have had more impact upon the travelling public.)

Thus was Midland Red (North) born, inheriting from its long-lived parent garages at Cannock, Stafford, Tamworth, Shrewsbury, Wellington and Ludlow. With these garages came 154 single-deck, 21 double-deck and 55 dual-purpose buses, a total of 230; details of the fleet at that date are in Chapter 9, Table 9.01. The new company was operating in a new environment and it had been made clear to the relevant county councils that services which did not cover their operating costs would only be maintained at a level appropriate to the financial support provided by the councils. Ian Mitchell, recently appointed by NBC, took office as Manager of the new company.

Some of the vehicles and operations which were included in the transfer of assets had come to the old Midland Red company in the latter part of the seventies by acquisition of two independent companies, Green Bus Company of Rugeley and, of greater import, Harper Brothers (Heath Hayes) Limited of Heath Hayes near Cannock. It was this second acquisition which gave the new company an operating base in South Staffordshire from which it was to grow in the ensuing years.

This, then, was typical of the situation across Midland Red when the split into the four 'compass point' bus companies occurred on 6 September 1981 and the new Midland Red (North) Limited commenced operation. John A Birks as General Manager had overseen the preparations for this most significant change in Midland Red and there is no doubt of the importance of his contribution in bringing to fruition the ideas of John B Hargreaves and John M Bodger together with his own; in the event he handed over as General Manager of Midland Red to Colin E Clubb some months before the actual dismantling of the company. It fell, therefore, to Mr Clubb to preside over the splitting into the six units and it was he who handed Midland Red (North) over to its new Manager, Ian Mitchell.

1 Paul Gray, Malcolm Keeley and John Seale; 'Midland Red' Volumes 1 and 2 (Transport Publishing Company, Glossop 1978, 1979).
2 Alan Townsin; 'The British Bus Story – Turbulent Times', (Transport Publishing Company, Glossop).
3 Doug Jack; 'Beyond Reality – the Twilight of Leyland Bus' (Venture Publications, Glossop 1994).
4 'National Bus Company 1968-1989', pp 186-187, (Transport Publishing Company, Glossop 1990).
5 Ibid, pp 325, 428
5a ibid, p 702.
5b ibid, pp 407-411

BMMO type S15 5073 is preserved by the Birmingham and Midlands Motor Omnibus Trust at Wythall. It spent all its life at Shrewsbury and was set up for the author's benefit in this form by kind co-operation of the museum.

Cannock garage in pristine condition at its opening in February 1977. The coach in National Express livery is an ex-Harpers Leyland Leopard/Plaxton, 2267 (PBF 199 M); other vehicles are one of the Midland Red type LS27 Leopards, an ex-Harpers Fleetline and two of the comparatively new Leyland Nationals.

Midland Red D9 5437 leaves Bradford Place, Walsall on a return trip to Stafford via Cannock. This was the remaining section of the long 65/865 Dudley-Tipton-Wednesbury-Walsall-Cannock-Stafford service which had been worked jointly with Walsall Corporation up to the sale of Midland Red's core to the West Midlands PTE. Gordon Weston

Leyland National 757, new in 1979, is seen leaving the Midland Red bus station in Birmingham on its way to Tamworth. It is in full NBC poppy red/white livery with the 'Mercian' local identity. This bus, with two others of the same vintage, went to Midland Red West in 1986.   Daniel Hill

6463 was one of only thirteen vehicles of BMMO type LS26, Leyland Leopards with Marshall B53 bodies new in 1972. It is seen at Pool Meadow ready for departure on service 545 to Market Harborough, a distance better suited to a dual-purpose vehicle. This bus passed to Midland Red South when MROC was split.

Midland Red type DD13 Daimler Fleetline 6191 spent all of its working life at Tamworth until its withdrawal in 1986.   John Senior

Chapter 2

Midland Red North up to Deregulation

Consolidation

Ian Mitchell, the Manager of the newly born Midland Red North, and his team reviewed the situation with which they were presented following the split-up of Midland Red Omnibus Company and sought to introduce their own ideas into the new company. Almost the first matter which was addressed was that of public perception. Certainly on 6 September 1981 it is unlikely that many of the travelling public noticed any difference, unless the more eagle-eyed perceived that the legal lettering on the buses had changed. As far as the ordinary passenger was concerned Midland Red had not changed, and that was not good news in view of the generally poor image which the company had unfortunately developed during the latter part of the 1970s. The decision was taken to focus upon the new local identities which were the product of the MAP schemes introduced shortly before the split. Each brand name had been given its own colour and it was decided to extend this colour identification by using a band of the appropriate colour on buses with the identity name in white. On single-deck buses the new colour bands replaced the standard white band at cantrail level, whilst on double-deck vehicles the same band was applied at waist level. The NBC 'double N' logo still appeared on a white square. The important change was the disappearance of the Midland Red name, except for legal lettering. It is interesting to compare the MRN action with what took place at sister company Midland Red (East); there the new management, also motivated by recognition of the poor image of the Midland Red name, renamed their company Midland Fox, as well as modifying the livery.

Ian Mitchell has commented that the method of setting up operating companies without the benefit of in-house financial management was a mistake and led to the very significant problems which beset Midland Red North in the ensuing years. The crunch came in 1984 when a modest operating profit became a substantial loss in the financial accounts. No one on the accountancy staff at PMT was ever able to identify the nature of the hole down which the profit had vanished. As will be seen in Chapter 4 this arms-length financial management made near-disaster after deregulation a virtual certainty.

(The situation was corrected in July 1986 when MRN was able to appoint a Finance Director, Fred Taylor, whose arrival and subsequent input have been described as the salvation of the company [6].)

Operating conditions in the new era were no easier than in the troubled 1970s. The growth of private motoring continued apace and passenger numbers and revenue were shrinking. The time was ripe for further change in an attempt to stem the drift. New initiatives were the order of the day as the management team endeavoured to change the pattern of decline.

Expansion

From 1981 to 1984 MRN pursued a policy of expansion based upon two distinct criteria. One element of the policy was to seek maximum local authority financial support of rural services. This policy was successful in the shorter term but, as is demonstrated in Chapter 3, it was to be an Achilles' heel for the company. With hindsight, as Ian Mitchell has commented, a better appreciation of the politics of the time might have led to an alternative strategy.

The other part of the expansion policy was to embark on new marketing initiatives. One of these involved joining the consortium of express services within the West Midlands conurbation branded as 'Midland Express' with the logo 'ME'; this caused some amusement amongst more cynical observers where it was suggested that there was perhaps some uncertainty within the company about its true identity. Another innovation was the setting up of a separate specialist coach hire unit, marketed as 'Rugeley Party Line'. Here the intention was to tap into the demand for small capacity coaches for day or evening private hire.

Taken in conjunction with the decision to promote vigorously local brand images there was created a completely new philosophy which bore little or no resemblance to that of the traditional regional bus company of preceding decades.

There were, of course, innovations which became victims of circumstances, and where there were lessons to be learnt. For example, MRN had started an express route, X86, from Stafford (Baswich) to Birmingham via the M6 Motorway in February 1982. This was intended to tap the commuter and shopping traffic between the two centres, traffic which was at the time captive to British Rail. Initially there were four return journeys per day, Monday to Saturday, with the first from Stafford at 0730 and the last from Birmingham at 1730 being timed to be of particular interest to the commuters.

The fares were extremely competitive with the contemporary rail fares and excited the interest of a group of rail season ticket holders. Being canny folk, however, they selected two of their number to run a trial for a week before committing themselves to forsake the railway. All was well for the Monday and Tuesday, the vehicle involved being a Leyland Leopard coach. Overnight on the Tuesday there was a sharp frost and Stafford garage thoughtfully provided a Leyland National bus which had been parked outside throughout the night. That one action, with the National's notorious 'cold feet' heating system, effectively ended the X86's brief career as a commuter service and it was not long before the early outward and late return journeys were dropped.

Even as a shopper's service the X86 failed to attract sufficient traffic and further cuts were made. On deregulation, with its associated retrenchment, Staffordian Travel took over the remnant of the service on tender to Staffordshire County Council; on subsequent tendering the X86 went to Stevensons with the service by now reduced to but one return journey per day. Interestingly, the wheel turned full circle when in September 1994 MRN regained control of the X86 under tender, introducing new features such as feeder services into Stafford from some of the outlying villages and a later return from Birmingham on Saturdays.

In tandem with the expansion policy running and maintenance costs were examined and one decision which was soon taken was to withdraw the fleet of Ford R192/ Plaxton buses. These lightweight buses had been introduced by Midland Red in 1970/1971 for use on rural routes. They had been seen as successors to the very sophisticated BMMO type S14, remarkable machines introduced in 1954 with disc brakes on all wheels, independent front wheel suspension and toggle link rear suspension. With an unladen weight of just over 5 tons the S14 was able to operate with single rear wheels, quite astonishing for a 44-seat bus of 30ft length. It is hardly surprising that the Fords never came up to the expectations of the operating or engineering departments.

The rapid withdrawal of the Ford R192s required the injection of replacements. Quantities of Leyland Leopard/ Marshall dual-purpose buses and Leyland Nationals were obtained from a number of sources, notably fellow Midland Red sector companies, Midland Red (East) and Midland Red (West). It is useful to note that NBC management of the time was coming to the conclusion that on a lifetime costing basis lightweight buses such as the Fords did not compare with heavy-duty types such as the Leyland Leopard or AEC Reliance [7].

The expansion policy required additional capacity. In 1983 the first new vehicles arrived. The intake included ten Leyland Olympians with ECW double-deck bodies to standard NBC requirements. There were also four Leyland Tigers with Plaxton Paramount high-floor coach bodies. For the first time since the earliest days new vehicles for a Midland Red company were registered in Staffordshire; they carried marks issued by the Local Vehicle Licensing Office in Stoke-on-Trent, underlining the location of the registered office of the company.

Three other new vehicles were part of the 1983 purchase. These were the mini-coaches for the new Rugeley Party Line marketing venture with bodywork by Reeve Burgess and based on Mercedes-Benz chassis. As it happened the exercise was not to prove a financial success for MRN and two had been disposed of by 1985, the third surviving just two more years.

All of the vehicles inherited from Midland Red Omnibus Company, and those obtained subsequently from fellow Midland Red sector companies, continued to carry their fleet numbers in the standard Midland Red single series,

with the exception of four Daimler Fleetlines inherited from the purchase of the Harper Brothers business and the former Stratford Blue Leyland Leopard. The Midland Red series had reached 6473 when a new series commencing at 101 was introduced in 1972, the first of the new series being a batch of the equally new Leyland Nationals. The new vehicles of 1983, however, introduced the beginning of a new numbering system which brought vehicles into separate series depending upon the type. Thus the mini-coaches were numbered 1-3; the Olympians carried the numbers 1901-1910, whilst the Tigers were in the range 1508-1511, these latter numbers reflecting the registrations allocated, A 508-511 HVT.

1983 saw a continuation of acquisition of buses and coaches from other NBC sources. These included more Leyland Nationals and Leyland Leopard dual-purpose vehicles from Midland Red (East), a selection of Leopard coaches and, significantly, four DMS-type Daimler Fleetlines from Western National, but originally from London Transport. A solitary Alexander bodied Fleetline was acquired from Trent Motor Traction, not too unlike vehicles of the same combination new to Midland Red.

In 1984 the process continued when further new vehicles were received. These comprised Leyland Tigers with bodies by Plaxton and Duple, to their 'Laser' design, and a further three Olympians with dual-purpose seated ECW double-deck bodies. An interesting purchase was the batch of nine Tigers with Duple Dominant bus bodies; the chassis were, however, to coach standards with high ratio rear axles. In addition the policy of bringing in further second-hand Leyland Nationals from other NBC companies continued with arrivals from Northern General. A second ex-Trent Daimler Fleetline was also acquired.

Undoubtedly the event of most interest, however, was the purchase of five MAN articulated buses which were originally intended for use by South Yorkshire PTE in Sheffield. These highly manoeuvrable buses, with seating for 53 passengers, were based at Cannock and operated from that garage for the next three years, usually on the 870 route to Wolverhampton. They were right-hand drive versions of the German VöV standard city bus of the 1970s, well constructed and robust. They suffered from but one disadvantage, apart from their non-standard features, in that they were too long to be accommodated within the bays at Cannock garage with the doors closed.

Ian Mitchell would have been happy to purchase new MAN buses of conventional rigid type built to the same German city bus standards but in spite of several requests for MAN to quote there was no positive response. It is instructive to consider how such vehicles would have compared with Leyland Nationals in service, and in particular in terms of longevity.

Full details of the vehicle acquisitions are given in Chapter 9.

Minibuses

National Bus Company had conducted an extensive study of the use of 16-seat minibuses by its Devon General subsidiary in Exeter. The project was initiated by John

Leyland National 515 (JOX 515 P) is seen in foreign territory at Telford near the end of its days with MRN. It was transferred to North Western just two weeks later in 1987. Wearing 'Hotspur' livery 515 had been on Shrewsbury's allocation but was spending its final days at Wellington.

Gordon Weston

Olympian 1907 sits at Delta Way in poppy red 'Chaserider' livery. It was one of the last vehicles to be outshopped in the NBC livery.

A scene from Cannock bus station in early MRN days shows ex- London Transport DMS Fleetline 1916 (TGX 831 M) about to depart for the improbably named Wimblebury. On the left sits one of the Midland Red standard Fleetlines with Alexander dual-entrance body whilst one of the MAN articulated buses loads for Rugeley. Geoffrey Smith

A night shot of ECW B51-bodied Leopard 1501 at the Tamworth Corporation Street terminal. In Midland Express livery it waits for departure time on service 110 to Birmingham via Sutton. It arrived from Southern Vectis in 1983 and was withdrawn in 1990 having been renumbered 1491 in 1988.

Les Simpson

Bridgnorth-based Leyland Tiger 1701, in poppy red 'Tellus' livery, arrives in the town on Telford area service 9.

Tamworth's first minibuses were PMT conversions of the ubiquitous Ford Transit. They appeared in what may be described as 'Mercian' Mark 1 minibus livery, yellow with green roof and skirt, edged in white. They also had destination blinds which were unusual for the time in having black lettering on an orange background. The 'Mercian' minibus logo was again in the local green.

Hargreaves, Derek Fytche and Brian Barrett in a paper to NBC in August 1983[8]. The perceived success of the exercise in Exeter prompted NBC management to advocate the wholesale introduction of similar minibus schemes in towns and cities throughout the country. MRN's first foray was in Stafford where nine new minibuses, based on the Ford Transit panel van and branded 'Chaserider Minibus', commenced operation of three completely new routes from the town centre to Baswich, Wildwood, Walton and Brocton to the south of the town. Full-size buses were completely replaced, apart from a few schools journeys, and for the first time there was bus access to parts of extensive residential areas [9].

50 more minibuses of the same type were acquired during the next year for introduction of minibus networks in Lichfield (27 March 1986), Telford and Shrewsbury (19 April) and Cannock (30 June). Tamworth commenced minibus conversion of the town services on 11 August with 18 Freight Rover/Dormobile minibuses.

The minibuses not only bore the local identity names which had been introduced by Midland Red in 1980 but also wore distinctive liveries which certainly made them stand out from their 'big bus' fellows, still wearing National Bus Company poppy red. Although the local identity colour, introduced by MRN shortly after its creation, was incorporated yellow was the main colour with sometimes a third colour band. Whatever opinions there were about this imaging it was undoubtedly eye-catching. The colour schemes for the minibus fleet, with their local identities, are given in detail in Chapter 6.

Undoubtedly the minibus initiative was an overall success, bringing bus access to areas of towns which had experienced either infrequent or irregular services from full-size buses or none at all. In the context of NBC operations in England and Wales the MRN experience was not in any way unusual. Ian Mitchell gave a paper to a professional meeting in 1986 which showed how effectively real passenger growth had been generated [9];

Town	Frequency increase	Passenger growth
Stafford	3 times	+80%
Shrewsbury	2 times	+40%
Lichfield	5 times	+100%

He also demonstrated how, after the introduction of minibuses in those same three towns, the percentage of costs met out of revenue had improved compared with the operation using full-size buses;

Percentage of Costs met from Revenue

Town	Before minibuses	After minibuses
Stafford	86	113
Shrewsbury	116	128
Lichfield	73	90

In the overall context it is clearly demonstrated that although the Lichfield venture gave a doubling of passenger usage the revenue still did not cover the costs of operation and thus it was inevitable that MRN would withdraw

operation. The results in Shrewsbury also gave some interesting information in that, although the minibus introduction did produce an increase in passenger journeys, the increase was not as dramatic as in Stafford and the improvement in the cost/revenue figure was again smaller. Indeed, in Shrewsbury the latter ratio had been acceptable for full-size buses in any case and in consequence the ultimate conversion to minibuses in that town was on a different scale from that in Stafford.

The approach of deregulation

As will be described later in Chapter 3 the impact of political thinking upon the bus industry was about to bring upheaval not only to Midland Red North but to the whole of the industry. It is sufficient to say at this juncture that Ian Mitchell and his colleagues were aware of the turmoil ahead and were planning to accommodate it. Indeed the policy of National Bus Company, including the splitting of the old Midland Red company, had taken account of the likely outcome of the return to power of a Conservative administration in the 1979 and 1983 elections. The policy of devolving much decision making to company managements was allowing them to examine their financial structures and operations in the light of likely radical changes to the industry at local level.

6   Interview with Ian Mitchell, 13 October 1994.
7   'National Bus Company' 1968-1989, p593, (Transport Publishing Company, Glossop 1990).
8   ibid, pp 440-443, 607-608.
9   (Author's note) The innovation was hailed in Stafford, as elsewhere, as a huge success, as indeed it was, with very significant increases in passenger numbers and route profitability. It is instructive to consider, however, how public opinion has changed since that time; 16-seat minibuses based upon short wheelbase van chassis have proven to be less than attractive to those with young children and shopping, and the trend to somewhat larger and more sophisticated vehicles is clearly evident ten years later (see Chapter 9).

Chapter 3

Deregulation and the Road to Privatisation

The political background

The Conservative Government returned to power in June 1983 had included in its election manifesto the promise to bring enhanced competition into public transport, by scrapping the system of licensing of services and operators introduced by the Transport Act 1930, reviewing the provision of subsidies for unremunerative services and seeking to remove operating entities from public ownership[10]. The key event in this context after the return of the Conservatives was the appointment of Nicholas Ridley as Secretary of State for Transport, in succession to Cyril Parkinson and Tom King, in October 1983. This was the man who would change the whole structure of the British bus industry by adopting a philosophy which will provoke argument for many years to come.

Ridley's first action was to publish a White Paper *'Buses'* in July 1984 which set out details of proposals putting flesh to the election promises. In January 1985 the Transport Bill was published which made provision for the abolition of road service licensing outside London, as from October 1986, and required local authorities and PTEs to go to open tender where subsidies were deemed to be necessary to support any local bus services.

Part III of the Bill dealt *inter alia* with the requirement for PTEs and district/regional councils which operated buses to transfer the assets to public transport companies which would operate at arms length from the relevant local authorities, and the privatisation of the National Bus Company and the Scottish Bus Group.

Despite intensive lobbying from many sectors of the industry there was little significant shift in Nicholas Ridley's position and with its unassailable majority the Government was able to push its Bill through both Houses of Parliament. The Transport Act 1985 was duly enacted on 30 October 1985.

26 October 1986 was set as the date when local bus services outside London would be deregulated whereby it became necessary only for a prospective operator to register the details of his intentions at that date to the Traffic Commissioners. There would then follow a period up to 25 January 1987 when operators were bound to continue to operate all registered services without variation. From 26 January 1987 the full impact of deregulation came into force, meaning essentially that any local service could be introduced, varied or withdrawn with notice of 42 days from the date of acceptance of registration by the Traffic Commissioner.

Services not registered commercially and deemed by the relevant local authority to have necessary social connotations were then to be put to open tender for support by the authority, the authority being bound to accept the lowest tender.

It was obvious that the four months from 30 October 1985, the date of enactment of the Transport Act, to the end of February 1986, the date for receipt of applications for registration of services to be operated from 'D-Day' as it became known, would be one of frenetic activity in the bus industry across the whole country. National Bus Company had prepared its subsidiaries well for this situation, but local service planning and licensing had always been a company matter. Their local managements now had much more autonomy and commercial responsibility and NBC headquarters had become rather like a holding company. Thus the identification for commercial registration of services and the submission of tenders for supported services was wholly at local level.

The experience of implementing service networks based on MAP analysis had provided much useful information to NBC subsidiaries and the identification of commercially viable services for registration was facilitated. Nevertheless the amount of work involved was considerable, particularly with respect to the restructuring of support income, where certain local authorities had anticipated the effects of the Act by changing the format of their subsidy arrangements before 'D-Day', with concomitant disturbance to planned cash flow for the operators concerned.

One other effect of the removal of the time-honoured regulation system of the previous half-century was that co-ordination of services between operators on shared routes and area agreements were to be terminated. Preparation for these changes simply added to the work-load. In MRN's case this latter requirement involved the arrangements with West Midlands PTE in the Cannock, Hednesford, Wolverhampton and Tamworth areas.

There was considerable restructuring of NBC up to the middle of 1986 and this has been described in detail in its official history [11]. Much of this restructuring was intended as NBC's response to the White Paper *'Buses'* where the Government had expressed its views on privatisation. Those views were essentially that it was inappropriate for a large national corporation to be the provider of local bus services. Using the success of the privatisation of the National Freight Corporation as the stimulus the Government proposed that National Bus Company be privatised, but in this case not as a single unit. NBC was prepared to identify how seven financially separate portfolio companies could be formed from its subsidiaries which could then be sold individually, the portfolios being constructed such that no two companies within the same portfolio would have contiguous territories. The advantage seen for portfolio management was that there would continue to be cohesion between operators in the same portfolio utilising appropriate economies of scale but without excessive local influence [12,13].

Ford Transit minibus 32 is very much a stranger in the camp in this scene at Lichfield bus station. It carries the designation 'Mercian' on the destination blind but wears the early 'Tellus' livery, yellow and dove grey with violet band. The time is likely to have been the introduction of minibuses to Lichfield in 1986 with the 'Tellus' Transit transferred in from Wellington.　　　　Daniel Hill

Dormobile bodied Ford Transit 99 (D 99 CFA) in almost new condition is seen at a location in Walsall. This was one of the minibuses which introduced MRN's post-deregulation incursion into the territory of West Midlands Travel.

Ridley would have none of it and went further to identify certain NBC subsidiaries which were in his opinion too large to allow for effective competition in their spheres of influence. He required, for example, that Ribble be split when the southern part was named North Western Road Car Company; the northernmost area was to be transferred to Cumberland, leaving Ribble with operations confined to central and northern Lancashire. Crosville was to have its Welsh operations split off as Crosville Wales, but including also the garage and operations at Oswestry and its various outstations. These two decisions were to have significance at a later stage for Midland Red North.

In May 1986 Nicholas Ridley was succeeded as Secretary of State for Transport by John Moore. There was no change in the Government's policies as far as the bus industry was concerned and events moved inexorably toward 'D-Day'. As it happened John Moore's tenure at the Department of Transport in Marsham Street was not destined to be a lengthy one; he was replaced by Paul Channon in June of the following year by which time the programme for disposal of the National Bus Company and its subsidiaries was in full swing. The first sale had taken place in July 1986 when National Holidays was sold to the Pleasurama leisure group; the first bus operator, Devon General, was sold to its management one month later. By the time Paul Channon came to office 34 operating companies, including 8 engineering companies, had already been sold.

Standing in what might be mistaken for a World War 2 bomb site is MRN 796, a Leyland Leopard with Willowbrook coach body to NBC specification. It was new in 1980. At the time of the photograph it was parked on the site being developed as Wolverhampton's new bus station wearing a garish livery for the short-lived 'Chaserider' express services introduced at deregulation. With others of the type 796 was a casualty of the 1987 purge. Daniel Hill

The scene at Delta Way following the decision to withdraw 104 buses and coaches in April 1987.
Charles Roberts

Deregulation

Although deregulation was set to become operative on 26 October 1986 Staffordshire County Council was one of those local authorities which took advantage of the coming situation which required open tendering for supported bus services. Acting on the prompting of its County Treasurer's Department, Staffordshire County Council took the view that from the commencement of the new 1986-1987 financial year they could anticipate the requirements of deregulation but without allowing Midland Red North to discontinue the level of service at the time. Clearly the intention was for the County Council to grasp an opportunity to save support cost short term without regard to the catastrophic effect which would impinge upon MRN's already fragile profitability[15]. It prompts the question whether local authorities ever have enough knowledge of,

or interest in, the welfare of commercial business in the community. This action by the local authority had the effect of wiping some half million pounds from the budgetted revenue support. Management action was able, however, to bring increases in other revenue of some 8.5% against increases in operating costs of 6% but the reduction in the revenue grant reduced overall revenue growth by 2%. The inevitable result was a worsening of the financial state of the company at the very time when it was having to face up to a hardening competitive environment.

Ian Mitchell's team had identified a number of possible areas of attack opened up by deregulation. Of particular interest is the skirmish with West Midlands PTE, by 1987 trading as West Midlands Travel.

At 'D-day' MRN introduced a number of express services in the Walsall and Wolverhampton areas. These included the following:

X1 Mossley Estate-Bloxwich-Walsall-Birmingham;
X32 Essington-Ashmore Park-New Invention-Birmingham;
X87 Wolverhampton-Stone Cross-Birmingham;
X89 Bridgnorth-Wolverhampton-Wednesfield-Willenhall-Birmingham.

A further foray followed with the registration of three routes in the Walsall area to be operated by minibuses. 29 brand new Ford 'New' Transits with Dormobile bodywork were to be employed, operating from an outstation in Queen Street, Walsall. The routes planned were Delves/Yew Tree to New Invention, Delves/Yew Tree to Ashmore Park, and Walsall to Wolverhampton via Darlaston, Willenhall and Bilston. The third service did not in fact commence until two weeks later; a heavy snowfall had interfered with the completion of driving tests and had led to a shortage of drivers at the planned commencement date.

West Midlands responded in vigorous fashion to protect an important part of its core business, the urban service networks connecting Walsall and Wolverhampton. Fares were reduced and a fleet of MCW Metroriders were put to work in keen competition with MRN's Transits. MRN was forced to retrench, by starting one hour later and finishing operation one hour earlier in the day, and by increasing off-peak fares. Clearly all was not well. Although the operation in Walsall was cash positive it was not achieving the level of profitability which MRN management knew they required. Consideration had to be given to the possibility that there were better returns to be made by putting resource elsewhere in the territory, and Telford was seen to be just such a case. Consequently the decision was made to withdraw and the service to Wolverhampton ceased on 15 August 1987 with the two others finishing on 6 September. The Transits were dispersed mainly to Wellington with a few to Stafford.

Like the Walsall/Wolverhampton minibus adventure the express services also fell by the wayside in the ensuing months. There had been plans to extend minibus operation into Wolverhampton but these were never activated following the experience in Walsall.

Prior to deregulation there had been a survey of opportunities for a minibus service network in Sutton Coldfield, these to be operated under the 'Mercian' banner. Once again the failure of the minibus initiative in Walsall to generate the required profit persuaded MRN's management to back away from further action of this type in West Midlands PTE territory. A point having been made, the brittle relationships between West Midlands and MRN were tempered somewhat, although the two operators continued to compete openly.

An interesting experiment took place in Lichfield where Midland Red had operated previously from a small garage between 1954 and 1971, when the vehicles based there were dispersed to the garages at Sutton, Tamworth and Swadlincote. On 27 March 1986 MRN returned to the city with a parade of 'Mercian' minibuses which were put into service two days later, on a free fare basis, in preparation

for commercial service on 1 April 1986. These minibuses were intended to replace full-size vehicles from Stafford and Tamworth garages on the city routes. The minibuses operated from a new garage in Station Road which was also used to house the 'Mercian' coaching unit.

In spite of considerable promotion the Lichfield minibus venture was not judged a success (see Chapter 2) and operations ceased on 13 April 1987. The four principal routes were taken over by Midland Fox and Stevensons. The garage premises were put up for sale, the new operators using a parking area at a local car dealer.

Fred Taylor was appointed as Finance Director of the company in July 1986. This event followed closely upon the transfer of the registered office from Woodhouse Street, Stoke-on-Trent to Delta Way, Cannock, all as part of the new NBC philosophy of devolving management down to operating subsidiary level. MRN was now able to manage itself effectively. By Christmas 1986 there was available sufficient management information to indicate that the earlier strategy for expansion in the West Midlands was not going to succeed in transforming the company's fortunes and that a change of tack was necessary. With the Government's policy of break-up of the National Bus Company now in train it was essential for the management team to revise its plans and indeed to decide whether it would be able to elicit financial backing for a management bid for the company.

Privatisation

David S. Winterbottom, at that time Deputy Chief Executive of Evode Group plc, had .been approached to act as non-executive chairman and financial adviser to the management team with the ultimate aim of involvement in constructing a management bid for purchase of the company under the government's privatisation programme. He had been involved in the appointment of Fred Taylor and now took a hand in assessing the financial problems of MRN in the post-deregulation era. If the company was to be in a fit state against which to secure support from financial institutions for a management buy-out the cost base would have to be drastically reduced.

The measures taken by the management team were in various ways draconian but perhaps the best remembered event of the time was what may be described as 'the night of the long knives' when on 26 April 1987, to the astonishment of the bus industry, 80 unprofitable bus operations were withdrawn with 200 associated redundancies; at the same time some 104 buses and coaches were withdrawn from service and offered for sale; this meant that in the first four months of that year a total of 113 vehicles were withdrawn. This action had the immediate effect of reducing operating costs and the value of capital assets with concomitant reduction in capital servicing costs on the balance sheet.

The prospectus document prepared by the management buy-out team gives a clear picture of the parlous state of the company in the mid-eighties. Much of the deteriorating performance in the years up to 1985 had been due to the coach operations, *viz*. private hire, excursions and tours.

The 1985 figures were affected by start-up costs associated with the introduction of the minibus operations and some £46 000 of the reported losses were attributed to this factor.

The following data have been extracted from a copy of that prospectus.

Year	Revenue, £000	Profit/(Loss), £000
1982	9 651	462
1983	10 340	255
1984	11 217	37
1985	11 910	(123)
1986	12 140	(591)

Operating costs had increased during the above period by 32% including a 22% increase in wages and national insurance.

The 1986 losses were particularly affected by the reduction in revenue support grants, a direct consequence of the 1985 Transport Act, and exacerbated by the manipulative actions of Staffordshire County Council as already described. From 1985 to 1986 these grants declined from £1.433 million to £870 000 of which £132 000 was the rural bus grant first introduced in 1986.

It must be said also that the 1986 figures were distorted by extraordinary items arising from additional depreciation, following revaluation of the fleet, and the redundancy costs consequent upon deregulation and deregistration.

After the first three months of the 1987 operating year there were already signs of improvement in that there was a favourable variance from the budgetted loss. The projections which were made in the management buy-out prospectus indicated that profit before interest charges and tax would move progressively from a deficit of £693 000 in 1986 to a positive £918 000 on a turnover of £10.265 million by 1989. It is interesting to compare these figures with the £1.783 million profit on a turnover of £13.283 million reported in the MRN accounts dated September 1988, results which then put MRN as the second most profitable ex-NBC company [14].

Bids for purchase of the company were required to be lodged by 3 June 1987. Initially there were five bidders with another two entering at the last minute. Visits were made by Allied Bus Services and Endless Holdings and bids from these two together with the management bid were the only survivors. On 20 August 1987 Allied Bus were declared successful in their bid for MRN as well as for East Midland Motor Services and Lincolnshire Road Car Company.

On 25 August there began a bizarre succession of events. Ian Mitchell, MRN's Managing Director, had met two executive directors of Allied Bus. Following this meeting Ian Mitchell had developed a concern about the intentions of Allied and advised the company and its advisers of his unwillingness to be associated with them in the event of the sale going through. When the delay in finalisation of the sale passed the six weeks timescale imposed by National Bus Company he wrote to NBC's senior negotiator and demanded that bidding should be re-opened. Ian Mitchell further expressed his views to the press, indicating that in his view Allied were merely speculating. He also referred to widespread rumour in the industry regarding 'links between Allied and another bidder for NBC companies' [15,16].

NBC Chairman, Rodney Lund, immediately suspended Ian Mitchell from duty. The row reached the floor of the House of Commons where a motion was tabled by Labour members deploring the possibility of Allied Bus being allowed to construct a virtual monopoly position extending across much of Central England [17].

NBC were ultimately convinced that there were indeed links between Allied Bus and Endless Holdings. Accordingly NBC required that bidding for the six companies which were to be sold to Allied and Endless Holdings be re-opened on 29 October 1987. Both companies were barred additionally from re-submitting bids [18,19].

Drawlane Transport Services Limited, in which Endless Holdings had a 25% stake, submitted a bid for Midland Red North. Five others, all former NBC companies, expressed interest but in the event only the bids from Drawlane and the management team were firm. On 1 December 1987 the Drawlane bid, £6.3 million, was declared successful. Completion of the sale was effected on 27 January 1988; both Ian Mitchell and Fred Taylor left immediately afterwards. Geoffrey Hilditch, a man with a lifetime of experience in the bus industry, adviser to Endless Holdings and Operations Director of Drawlane, was then installed as caretaker Managing Director, taking responsibility for a company with 248 vehicles, 491 employees and five principal garage properties.

10 National Bus Company 1968-1989', Chapter 2, pp 133-134 (Transport Publishing Company, Glossop 1990).
11 *ibid*, Chapter 10.
12 *ibid*, pp 674-675.
13 *ibid*, Appendix Three.
14 'Bus Business', 13 December 1989, p9.
15 Interview with Ian W. Mitchell, 13 October 1994.
16 'Bus Business', 21 October 1987, p1.
17 Hansard, Notices of Motions: 23 October 1987, No. 175
18 'National Bus Company 1968-1989', Chapter 10, pp 676-678 (Transport Publishing Company, Glossop 1990).
19 'Bus Business', 4 November 1987, pp 1, 20.

Two Leyland Nationals at Delta Way in different forms of Geoffrey Hilditch's corporate livery style for Drawlane companies. On the left is former MRN 516 in Shamrock and Rambler white/green whilst 596 sports the new white/red for MRN. Charles Roberts

Former MRN 809, a Leyland National 2, demonstrates the diagonal three colour livery of North Western. Charles Roberts

Chapter 4

Into the British Bus Era

Beginnings

The purchase by Drawlane brought with it an injection of new management. Geoffrey Hilditch had acted as Managing Director from the acquisition date but it was clear that this would not be a permanent appointment. No attempt was made at that time to replace Fred Taylor as Financial Director, the financial control of the company being vested in Bob Hodgetts as Company Secretary with support from Drawlane headquarters in Salisbury. Les Birchley, who had been Fleet Engineer from 1981 and then Operations Manager, had left at the end of 1987 to join Badgerline, to be succeeded by Les Warneford who joined the company from Grimsby-Cleethorpes Transport.

Geoffrey Hilditch's son, Chris Hilditch was to be appointed Operations Director and the intention was that Bob Gregory, at the time Traffic Manager at North Western, would come in as Managing Director. As it happened, however, the incumbent MD David Foster left North Western and Bob Gregory was named his successor, a train of events which led to Chris Hilditch becoming Managing Director of Midland Red North. Les Warneford, who would have reported to Chris Hilditch as Operations Director, then succeeded to that position himself.

The fluidity in management appointments continued in succeeding years. Bob Hodgetts moved within the Drawlane group to become Financial Director with London Country (South West) and he was succeeded by Rob Williams. In 1991 Les Warneford rejoined Grimsby-Cleethorpes Transport as Managing Director.

Hardly surprisingly there was much local concern that the new owners of Midland Red North, with apparently scant experience of bus operation, might indulge in asset stripping. Drawlane management were at pains to refute such suggestions and strenuously argued through the media that their intentions were to bring effective management to the company such that it could then benefit from profitable operations and injection of capital in the form of new buses. As with all NBC subsidiaries in the run up to privatisation MRN had virtually abandoned its normal vehicle replacement policy as a means of containing the asset value on the books and, therefore, the value of the company. The result was that the fleet, with the exception of the minibuses, had a higher age profile than was desirable and this in itself was a factor which did not escape the notice of local politicians.

Immediately after acquisition Geoffrey Hilditch embarked upon a series of measures designed to emphasise the change of ownership and to set the scene for projection of Drawlane as a serious group in the bus industry. One of his ideas was for a corporate style of livery which would nevertheless avoid the blanket requirements of the erstwhile NBC style or the totally rigid approach adopted by the rapidly growing Stagecoach concern. It is said that his draft design was put together while on a journey by rail to Torquay. The progress of development of this 'corporate' style in the case of Midland Red North is described in detail under 'Liveries' in Chapter 6. It is sufficient for this part of the story to state that there were several changes of direction before anything like a standard was achieved.

As a postscript to the corporate livery style saga it is pertinent to comment that although London Country (South West) adopted an attractive two-tone green and red version designed by Ray Stenning, another of Drawlane's principal subsidiaries, North Western, had opted for a red, blue and white diagonal scheme inspired by consultants Haydon Hyphen prior to being bought by Drawlane. It was then clear that Drawlane management was not inclined to apply too much corporate muscle to its subsidiaries. In 1994, however, due to a change of managing director who took an instant dislike to the diagonal scheme, even North Western was disposed to change its livery to a more conventional application of its three colour scheme.

The fortunes of Drawlane companies varied significantly in the new era of deregulation. Whilst London Country (South West), to be better known a little later as London and Country, was developing a successful business by grafting newly acquired London Regional Transport tendered services onto its traditional network Shamrock and Rambler was suffering badly in its efforts to wrest traffic from Bournemouth Transport in that town. A high frequency minibus network had been introduced to capture passengers from the incumbent but Bournemouth's response had been extremely effective. The Shamrock and Rambler fleet of minibuses, operating as Charlie's Cars, was withdrawn and dispersed to other Drawlane companies, Midland Red North being one recipient. The full-size bus fleet of the Shamrock and Rambler company was dispersed likewise as Drawlane decided that the south coast based company should cease trading and again some of these came to Cannock.

Drawlane companies, North Western Road Car Company and Midland Fox were trading successfully. In the Manchester area, where former NBC Chairman Robert Brook had been involved with United Transport in setting up a minibus network to compete with GM Buses, Bee Line Buzz Company, Stagecoach Group subsidiary Ribble and Drawlane's North Western were also in contention. Through a series of *quid pro quo* arrangements United Transport withdrew from Preston, North Western withdrew from Blackburn and Ribble conceded South Manchester. United Transport decided to withdraw from bus operations completely and the Bee Line business was sold to Drawlane. To complete the complex picture it is necessary to look at the history of Crosville, a much admired former Tilling company within National Bus Company ownership, and its involvement with Drawlane; that part of the story is told separately in Chapter 5.

Above: A comparison in Drawlane style liveries is afforded by this view of two East Lancs double-deck buses. The nearer is Dennis Dominator 1802 whilst the one in yellow/red livery is Leyland Olympian 1919.

Former National Travel West Leopard 1503 (SLJ 386 X) looks well with its Plaxton Supreme body in the yellow/red Drawlane livery, although still devoid of fleetnames.   Daniel Hill

A new type of minibus arrived in 1991. These were eleven of the 23- seat Renault S56/NCME combination acquired from North Western. One of the batch, 342 (E 92 WCM) was destroyed in the fire at Stafford garage.

In 1991 MRN received six of a batch of almost new Dennis Falcons with East Lancs EL2000 bodies from fellow Drawlane company London and Country. 1210 (G 310 DPA) gleams in the sunlight at Delta Way, lettered 'Tellus Midland Red' ready for delivery to Wellington.

The scene at Pilgrim Place garage on the morning after the fire in the early hours of 2 February 1992. The remains of Ford Transit 23 lie at the exit doors.
Geoffrey Smith

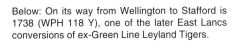

Below: On its way from Wellington to Stafford is 1738 (WPH 118 Y), one of the later East Lancs conversions of ex-Green Line Leyland Tigers.

Consolidation

During the first years of Drawlane ownership there was considerable movement of vehicles between its operating subsidiaries. There was an exchange of Leyland Nationals with London Country (South West), some MRN standard types going south with a number of the same as well as the first of the B series coming north to Cannock. Similar exchanges took place with North Western involving MRN's National 2 batch going north.

There was concern to examine alternative minibuses to those based upon Ford Transit chassis. Under NBC ownership the 16-seat Freight Rover Sherpa with Dormobile conversion had been acquired for use on a foray into Derby which actually commenced in July 1988. Subsequently agreement was reached whereby MRN secured a share of the equity of Derby City Transport (by transferring to Derby its fleet of Freight Rover Sherpa minibuses) and terminated its activities in February 1990. In return Derby withdrew from its corresponding incursion into MRN's territory in Tamworth some six weeks later.

Further examples of Freight Rover chassis with Carlyle bodywork were obtained new or from North Western and Shamrock and Rambler, including a few with the extended 20-seat capacity; apart from one, these higher capacity minibuses were not included in the Derby exercise and remained with MRN. Other minibus designs acquired included a batch of new Iveco-Fiat 49-10 vehicles with Carlyle bodies in 1989 together with Dormobile bodied Freight Rovers, the latter going subsequently to Derby.

The move away from the Ford Transit continued with further Freight Rover and Iveco 49-10 acquisitions from Crosville Wales and Bee Line; a batch of eleven Renault S56/Northern Counties buses with 23 seats arrived from North Western along with a further seven new vehicles of the same combination. It is perhaps fair to point out that these moves were inspired more by a need to have vehicles with seating capacity in excess of the sixteen or eighteen seats of the Transits than by any disenchantment with Ford. Indeed the original Transits of 1985 were still performing satisfactorily beyond the lifetime anticipated by NBC at the time of their introduction in the mid-eighties and further examples were acquired, both new and second-hand, into the 1990s.

One design which appeared in the fleet in 1990 was the Renault-Dodge S46 with Northern Counties 22-seat body. A number of this combination, new to United Transport's Manchester Minibuses Limited (Bee Line Buzz Company), arrived between 1991 and 1993, some from North Western and some via Bee Line or C-Line. These vehicles were not liked by the operating department having more than their fair share of reliability problems.

On the full-size bus side there were numerous transfers into MRN from other Drawlane subsidiaries. Whilst some of these were Leyland Nationals there were also Leyland Leopard coaches and dual purpose types. The sources were North Western or Shamrock and Rambler. Also from Shamrock and Rambler came two MCW Metroliner double-deck coaches which had originally been purchased for National Express workings; these were similar to the solitary Metroliner purchased by MRN in 1986 but which was a casualty in the 'night of the long knives' episode of April 1987. Again the reader is referred to Chapter 9 for full details of additions to and eliminations from the fleet.

There was much activity in terms of evaluation of demonstrator vehicles and this part of the subject is dealt with in some detail in Chapters 9 and 10.

The acquisition of the two parts of the former Crosville business brought an influx of buses to Midland Red North. Of particular significance was the number of Bristol VRT/ECW double-deck buses, a combination which had never been purchased by Midland Red. For whatever reason these buses, like the Renault-Dodge S46 minibuses, did not find favour with their new owners and although at the end of 1994 a few remained in service the type was clearly earmarked for early elimination. The vehemence of MRN repugnance of the Bristol VRT seemed to echo the opinions from Midland Red's Carlyle Works 25 years earlier.

The need for updating of the fleet was approached from two angles. Apart from the steady influx of new minibuses there were small batches of Leyland Olympian and Dennis Dominator double-deck buses followed by two batches of Dennis Falcon rear- engined single-deck buses arrived, the first being six which were transferred virtually new from London and Country. All of these were bodied by East Lancs Coachbuilders, a fellow Drawlane company.

The other approach to the vehicle replacement problem was to search for a batch of good second-hand buses which, with rebodying, might be expected to have a further ten years life. Such vehicles were identified with London Country (South West), a batch of Leyland Tigers with ECW coach bodies which had been purchased for Green Line duties. The story of their revitalisation is told in Chapter 8.

The policy of Drawlane from the outset was to secure its position within its operating territories by vigorous competitive action, including seeking as much tendered support revenue as deemed prudent. This strategy was noticeably at variance with what had been Ian Mitchell's firm belief that the future for the business lay in concentration upon commercially viable services alone.

A development in the post-privatisation years was the appearance of what might be described as cross-trading between the major new groupings. Reference has been made already to the rationalisation of services and operators in South Manchester. The minibus initiative in Walsall and Wolverhampton early in 1987, planned before the sale of MRN to Drawlane, had not borne fruit and in the face of stiff retaliatory action from West Midlands Travel MRN had pulled out just seven months later. The result was an armed truce between the parties which has continued.

Conflict with Williamsons Motorways in Shrewsbury town was resolved more or less amicably by MRN restricting its competitive action on Williamson's traditional routes to Meole Village, although MRN has retained some activity with a single route. A similar situation occurred in the Cannock area where there developed some fierce fare cutting between MRN and the local independent, Warstone of Great Wyrley, better known by its trading name Green Bus Service. In 1991 the parties agreed to respect each other's traditional core routes and the conflict ceased.

A key element throughout the territory has been to secure county support wherever possible and in particular for off-peak and Sunday services for those routes which are operated commercially for a substantial part of the working week. This is seen as an important component of strategy by keeping competitive action on the core route network to a minimum and has been pursued vigorously and successfully in Staffordshire, Shropshire, Cheshire, Powys and Clwyd.

Two local independents in the Stafford area, Greatrex and Happy Days Travel, entered into negotiations with MRN in 1991 with a view to selling their stage carriage interests. Both companies were suffering financially in the difficult times following deregulation when the situation was worsened by the slowdown in the national economy. Greatrex and Happy Days were restructured and operations were vested in a new company, Staffordian Travel, but with the Happy Days trading name retained for Woodseaves-based activities. The Staffordian stage carriage business to Great Haywood and Hixon was acquired on 29 July 1991, but without any vehicles involved. The Happy Days stage carriage business, in western Staffordshire and Shropshire, was acquired on 21 October 1991 together with three new Scania K93CRB/Plaxton buses, one Mercedes/Alexander midibus and one Ford Transit minibus. The two then inter-related businesses of Staffordian and Happy Days continued with private hire, extended tours and schools contract work.

Within a short time MRN took the opportunity to rationalise the services which it had inherited by these two deals. Of particular significance was the creation of a through service, 481, linking Stafford with Telford and Wellington via Newport, which commenced operation in February 1992. Connections were provided initially at Wellington for Shrewsbury but subsequently service 519 Newport-Crudgington-High Ercall-Shrewsbury was re-timed to provide a more convenient connection between Stafford and Shrewsbury.

An event of real significance occurred during the very early morning of 2 February 1992 when Stafford garage at Pilgrim Place was consumed by fire. Arson has always been suspected but the police have been unable to identify any culprits. In all 20 buses were destroyed with some less serious damage to others. But for the valiant efforts of a handful of employees vehicle losses would have been much higher.

The fire could not have come at a more difficult time. Later that same day the centre of Stafford was being pedestrianised with no access to buses. All routes were affected and in normal operating conditions there would have been problems for the operating staff. With a magnificent contribution from the whole workforce replacement buses were called in from all other garages during the early hours of that Monday morning such that the new traffic arrangements went into effect without any hitch.

Facilities were made available to MRN at the former site of BRC Engineering at Silkmore Lane, Stafford. This was a custom-designed factory which had produced drawn structural steel reinforcement and the buildings were therefore arranged with long uninterrupted bays. Stafford operations immediately moved into what would be their home until the construction of a new garage in the town; it was soon decided that the Pilgrim Place garage would not be rebuilt, because of the difficult access, and the site was sold for redevelopment.

Initially Silkmore Lane was simply a dormitory garage, with all maintenance and repair work carried out at Delta Way, Cannock. Within a few months, however, Stafford had been set up to carry out all its own support work. The borrowed buses, still with their 'foreign' local identities, gradually returned to their home bases. The main effect of the fire and the attendant shortage of vehicles was that a number of buses due for withdrawal were reprieved for some months.

The independent King Offa Travel had operated buses and coaches in parts of Shropshire, including a local service in Shrewsbury. In 1992 MRN acquired the town service business, which became MRN service 26, Bus Station-Reabrook Estate. With this acquisition came three Freight Rover/Carlyle minibuses.

Richard Bowler replaced Chris Hilditch as Managing Director in October 1992. One of his first actions was to look at what had become a somewhat shabby image for MRN. The final version of the Drawlane corporate style, with the mainly white body, was attractive when outshopped but, like so many white-based liveries, it weathered badly. (It is the author's opinion that the specification for the paint scheme may have been deficient and certainly the absence of a varnish finish coat, particularly on white, can be a recipe for trouble.)

On his arrival Richard Bowler noted that each garage had been allocated one bus painted in a facsimile of the traditional pre-war livery of Midland Red, even to the fleetname in shaded gold roman lettering. This had been the result of a suggestion from grass roots level for the celebration of the diamond jubilee of the opening of the original Charlton Street garage at Wellington in 1932. He immediately discussed with his staff the possiblity of having the red livery introduced as the standard. From that moment there was an enthusiastic response and arrangements were made for the change-over to be executed in as short a time as finances would permit.

Stevensons has been a keen competitor in various parts of MRN's territory since deregulation, appearing in Stafford, Cannock, Rugeley, Lichfield, Wolverhampton, Telford and Macclesfield. Open struggle was tempered by the share exchange between Stevensons and Midland Fox, followed by the acquisition of the latter by Drawlane Transport Group. The situation was further complicated by Stevensons' aggressive attack upon West Midlands Travel in parts of the Black Country and even within the City of Birmingham. WMT responded in 1994 by taking the battle into Stevensons, own heartland of Burton-on-Trent, where Stevensons had taken over the town service

Stevensons 97 was one of a pair of Leyland Olympians with Alexander RL bodies new in 1988. It is seen in Burton-on-Trent working a diagram on the 112 service to Birmingham, formerly a Midland Red route operated from Sutton and Swadlincote garages.   Gordon Weston

514 was one of the first Dennis Darts of 1994 to be delivered to Stafford. It stands at the temporary garage at Silkmore Lane bound for duty on the 76 town service.

Williamsons secured the first Shrewsbury Park and Ride contract. This operates to and from Harlescott on the northern edge of the town. One of the Carlyle bodied Dennis Darts used on this service is seen in High Street.

One of the Midland Red North Dennis Darts purchased for the Shrewsbury Park and Ride contract loads at the bus station for Harlescott Grange. It is on normal town service work, being only required for the Meole Brace P+R contract on Fridays and Saturdays.

network from the district council some years earlier; WMT used buses from its low-cost 'Your Bus' operation. Stevensons, faced with a contest which they could never win, agreed to sell their business to British Bus in August 1994; through the inheritance of the Midland Fox holding, British Bus already had a sizeable stake. Once again the *quid pro quo* routine was invoked; Stevensons withdrew from West Midlands territory and WMT's 'Your Bus' subsidiary went home from Burton.

Relationships between MRN and Stevensons then operated on a closer basis, with the Delta Way facilities available for servicing of buses based at the Stevensons Rugeley garage. Within a few weeks some Stevensons vehicles were actually transferred to MRN strength, and in MRN red livery. The tenuous existence of the MRN outstation at Etruria was rationalised in November 1994 when the services operated from there, with the exception of the C84 Hanley-Crewe-Chester, were transferred to the Stevensons unit at nearby Burslem and Etruria was closed.

Richard Bowler had moved to a more senior position within British Bus, the renamed Drawlane, in the summer of 1994, but retained his involvement with MRN as Executive Chairman. His place as Managing Director went to Keith Rogerson who had been hitherto Financial Director at Cannock.

British Bus, having been restructured, was now in a position to expand, both by acquisition and by investment in new vehicles. 1994 saw the results of the latter with the arrival of a batch of 22 Dennis Dart midibuses with fully automatic transmission followed by a batch of 12 Mercedes-Benz 811D midibuses. The move to midibuses was welcomed by the travelling public who had long since tired of the novelty of Ford Transit derived minibuses.

When in 1990 Shrewsbury and Atcham District Council together with Shropshire County Council indicated their intention to introduce Park and Ride facilities for Shrewsbury, MRN and Williamsons Motorways submitted tenders for the scheme which provided for a parking area at the Harlescott Livestock Market connected to the town centre by a frequent bus service operating Monday to Saturday. Although MRN had prepared a Dennis Dart/East Lancs vehicle for the tender the decision went against them and the contract was awarded to Williamsons. This caused some ill-feeling at MRN's local offices since the unplanned effect was that, since the car park was unmanned, some of MRN's passengers forsook the commercial service buses from Harlescott to use the subsidised P+R service with its cheaper return fare to the town centre.

In November 1994, however, a second opportunity was afforded MRN when the local authorities, pleased with the results of the Harlescott P+R scheme, sought to introduce another Monday to Saturday service connecting Meole Brace with the town centre. On this occasion MRN were successful and introduced four Dennis Darts with Marshall bodies to the specification of the county council. These were painted in a special livery of blue and yellow, incorporating the arms of the county and district councils, with the legend 'Shrewsbury Park and Ride'.

The terms of the contract were for the four buses to be available on Fridays and Saturdays. For the rest of the week only two vehicles were required and so it became possible on those days to see a P+R bus on standard town services, even on the 9, Shrewsbury Bus Station-Harlescott Grange.

The final act in the development of Midland Red North, as far as this story is concerned, took place on 1 January 1995 when the Macclesfield based services and garage passed yet again to another British Bus constituent company. This time the recipient was Stevensons which already had an operation in the Macclesfield area.

Even in December the signs of change could be seen at Sunderland Street, with a profusion of buses in the yellow livery of Stevensons.

As a postscript to the story, and an indication of how MRN has established itself in the world of privatised bus companies, the revenue for the year ended December 1993 was £17.243 million with a profit before tax of £1.593 million. When compared with the figures for 1988 quoted in Chapter 3, however, it becomes obvious just how hard the industry has to fight to make profit for growth and investment.

Chapter 5

The Crosville Inheritance

Crosville, in common with much of the bus industry, had experienced industrial relations problems at several of its depots during the 1970s and 1980s. The arrival of deregulation after the passing of the 1985 Transport Act merely highlighted the problem in certain areas. One such was Crewe where Crosville had registered comparatively little of its service network. PMT gained significantly in the Crewe area on subsequent tendering, and with some initial success. Crosville came to the inevitable conclusion that with the business based on Crewe now at a much reduced level Crewe garage and bus station were no longer viable financially. The decision was made to vacate the garage premises and move the operations to a low cost unit at Crewe Gates Industrial Estate, in effect an outstation. The garage was not, however, sold but merely mothballed. The bus station was retained with charging out to other operators, an innovation allowed by the 1985 Act.

The requirement of the Secretary of State for Transport for what were seen to be 'larger' National Bus Company subsidiaries to be split ahead of privatisation had meant that Crosville was to be so treated. Indeed the Secretary of State, the late Nicholas Ridley later Lord Ridley, took the unprecedented step of defining how the split was to be arranged. The whole of the Welsh operations together with those based on Oswestry were to become vested in a new company, Crosville Wales Limited whilst the remainder of the business would continue as Crosville Motor Services Limited.

After the split, which was effected in 1986, Crosville Wales was sold to its management in December 1987. Crosville Motor Services Limited was then sold to ATL (Western) Holdings Limited in March 1988. Subsequently the privatised National Express bought Crosville Wales from its new owners in January 1989 whilst Crosville Motor Services was sold by ATL to Drawlane Transport Group Limited.

Drawlane was faced with a problem of balancing revenue from its acquisitions against the associated costs, having backed away from wholesale sell-off of properties as a means of raising cash, because of the marked drop in property values. One consequence which is germane to this story was a decision to split up Crosville Motor Services in an endeavour to reduce operating and management costs whilst retaining as much revenue as possible within the Group. The operations centred on Crewe and Etruria became part of MRN and these were identified under the 'Midland Red Line' branding; the garage at Crewe was then re-opened. Some urgently required remedial work was carried out on the bus station forecourt. The Red Line management offices were sited at the bus station.

The operations at Runcorn, Warrington and Northwich were transferred by Drawlane to its North Western Road Car Company. At the same time the Macclesfield and Congleton garages and services had been brought under the management of yet another Drawlane subsidiary, Bee Line Buzz Company. The identity 'C-Line' with a livery style somewhat reminiscent of Crosville was applied at that time to the Macclesfield/Congleton operation. Another operating base at Hulme Hall Road in Manchester was used for the Bee Line and C-Line operations.

Macclesfield garage, opened with the adjacent bus station in 1939, had been operated by the original North Western Road Car Company and passed to Crosville on 1 January 1972 when that undertaking was split up in the aftermath of the formation of SELNEC PTE, the body set up to co-ordinate passenger transport in the Greater Manchester area. This same action had also brought Biddulph and Northwich into Crosville ownership, the latter passing to the 'new' North Western under Drawlane ownership some eighteen years later. Biddulph was a jointly operated garage owned by PMT and closed on its initiative, leading to Crosville opening an outstation at Congleton in 1982; this outstation, sited at the cattle market, then came into C-Line ownership.

Further west, meantime, Drawlane had bought a stake in Crosville Wales by a somewhat circuitous route. Crosville Wales, formed in 1986 by Ridley's enforced division of Crosville Motor Services, had been acquired by National Express in January 1988. National Express was sold by its management owners to a shelf company, Speedtheme Limited, in July 1991; Drawlane held a minority share in Speedtheme which was a vehicle for the forthcoming flotation of National Express. Speedtheme then immediately sold Crosville Wales to another shelf company, Catch Deluxe which was also associated with Drawlane. When National Express was floated on the stock market in mid-1992 Crosville Wales became a fully owned subsidiary of British Bus plc, Drawlane's successor. The name British Bus, incidentally, had been owned by National Express and was sold to Drawlane for £1000.

Crosville Wales had experienced industrial problems at its Wrexham garage during 1991, culminating in a damaging strike. The management took action to dismiss the strikers and close the Wrexham garage, with dispersion of activities to its Mold and Oswestry garages. Drawlane, which was by then managing Crosville Wales, decided upon rationalisation of operations and transferred the Oswestry garage with its outstation at Abermule to MRN in December 1991. The local branding 'Cambrian Midland Red' was applied by MRN to these inherited operations. The first change in management structure saw the Abermule outstation pass to Shrewsbury control. By 1993 Oswestry had also become part of the Shrewsbury management area.

The C-Line entity was transferred to the management

of MRN on 1 January 1993. One of the first actions of MRN was to transfer in three Scanias which had been acquired with the stage carriage interests of Happy Days Travel, in standard white/red/yellow livery and with the identity 'C-Line Midland Red'. It was thus evident that MRN would not only manage C-Line but would apply its own identity and livery to the Macclesfield-based operation. The reason for avoiding total integration of C-Line at that time was that the operating licences were issued by the North Western Traffic Area in the name of C-Line, whereas all of MRN's other activities, except Crewe, and its registered office, were in the West Midlands Traffic Area.

The shared premises in South Manchester were transferred wholly to Bee Line Buzz Company in April 1993 together with the C-Line vehicles based there. With the responsibility for Congleton transferring to Crewe in June 1993 the vehicles based there became technically 'Midland Red Line' operated.

The administrative problem over operating licences was ultimately resolved when these were transferred to the name of Midland Red North and C-Line became simply an operating area, with local management located at Macclesfield bus station, the transfer taking place in January 1994. With the fading of local identities, consequent upon the introduction of the 'Midland' corporate livery, Congleton moved back to being an outstation of Macclesfield later in 1994. Then in November of the same year there was further change. Congleton was closed and the vehicles there transferred to Crewe whilst on 1 January 1995 Macclesfield and its operations were transferred to fellow British Bus company, Stevensons.

Author's note:
Much of this chapter is based upon discussions with David J. Meredith, former Managing Director of Crosville Motor Services. He has cleared up many misconceptions and has brought a sensible understanding to what was a rather complicated part of the story. For all of this the author is indebted to him.

This is pure nostalgia. Preserved North Western Tilling Stevens DB 5070 is manoeuvering at a rally, showing route boards for the Manchester-Macclesfield service, still operated in 1994 as Midland Red North 129/130.
Pullman Preservation

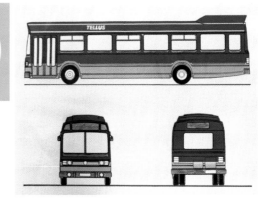

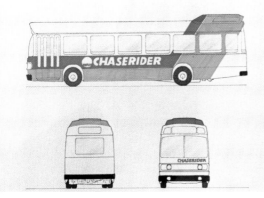

Upper left: A selection of the first design studies offered by livery consultants WDM.

Upper right: To continue the theme of the first concept sketches the agency produced a set of two-and three-colour livery designs where the principal colour in each case was the brand colour of the local identity. One example is shown.

Upper centre: Incorporated in the final set of design proposals was the 'badge' of the company, a solid red disc inscribed in white with 'MRN'.

Left: Subsequent to the initial discussions attention focused on the idea of a mainly white body colour with the then fashionable diagonal band treatment in bright colours. One of the proposals which did not make it is shown.

Left: Leyland National 653 (PUK 653 R) was the recipient of another of the candidate livery schemes considered in the run-up to privatisation. Fortunately none of these survived long. Charles Roberts

Below: 764 (BVP 764 V) was one of the last batch of Leyland National 11351A type, new in 1980. It is seen on local service work in Tamworth on a fine summer day in 1994, decked out in 'Midland' red.

filler point and at the rear. Later the large grey numbers were replaced by smaller characters in grey and then in black at those same positions.

The incongruity of having livery schemes which allowed minibuses and dual purpose full-size buses to share the same image was soon realised. When the original minibus logo was finally replaced by the standard style of fleetname the confusion was merely enhanced. Thus it was decided by 1990 that minibuses would be painted in the same three colour format as normal buses, with the predominantly white treatment. Tamworth was, of course, the exception but it also has to be said that at garages other than Cannock and Stafford the rate of change was slow, to the extent that even in 1994 minibuses at Shrewsbury could still be seen in the mainly yellow version of the three colour scheme [22].

The return to 'Midland' red

The next major event in the saga of liveries occurred in 1992 when, to mark the sixtieth anniversary of the opening of Charlton Street garage, Wellington, it was decided by the operations staff there to have one of their Leyland Tiger/Duple Dominant buses decked out in a version of the Midland Red livery of 1932 complete with gold lining. 1705 emerged in magnificent shape from the Delta Way paintshops to startle the local populace in Telford.

Immediately the decision was taken, as a promotional venture, to paint one vehicle from each garage in this style. Tamworth had one of its Leyland Olympian/ECW double deckers so treated while Stafford's example was a recently 'de-podded' Leyland National, 969. The choice for Cannock was one of the East Lancs rebodied Leyland Tigers, 1713. Since this bus was equipped with dual purpose seating it was given the black roof characteristic of BMMO practice for such vehicles and it was paraded in that format at an open day at Delta Way on a glorious summer day in 1992.

The buses carried the gold 'Midland' fleetname, in shaded roman characters, on each side and, with the exception of the Wellington-based Tiger, the traditional BMMO garter, inscribed ' 'Midland Red' Motor Services', on the rear panel. The Wellington bus had a different rear-end decoration, a garland enclosing the words 'Diamond Jubilee'. Fleet numbers in shaded gold characters of the block style used by BMMO appeared on the front dash and rear panels and in small black helvetica characters at the fuel filler point.

Certainly this was a success as a promotional exercise. Favourable comment was received from a wide range of sources, many of which would normally have had little interest in bus liveries. Perhaps the most significant, however, was the reference to the initiative by John Mervyn Pugh in his Presidential Address to the Omnibus Society in 1993.

One of new Managing Director Richard Bowler's first actions was to look at the image which was presented by the company. He saw an ageing fleet, apart from the minibuses, with a mainly white livery style which suffered badly from the effects of weathering. He also saw the need for something which would rekindle identification with and some enthusiasm for the 'Midland Red North' name. The

Wellington anniversary livery came to his notice and immediately he expressed the view that to adopt the red 'Midland' livery style could revitalise the company and give it and its staff a new identity.

Consequently a programme was put in train to re-paint the fleet in as short a time as could be afforded, given the financial strictures upon a bus company in the 1990s. The initial target was to have this completed by the end of 1994, but that turned out to be somewhat ambitious. Nevertheless the rate of change was sufficiently rapid to ensure that by the summer of 1994 one was more likely to see the red livery than its predecessors. It is inevitable that in an exercise of this sort, with a wide range of vehicle types ranging from minibuses to full-size double deckers, it is difficult to ensure uniformity of interpretation. Thus, gold lining application varied in terms of position, even with otherwise identical buses. Fleet number application likewise was subject to confusion. An early repaint was Stafford's East Lancs bodied Tiger 1724 which appeared with a black roof, even though it had normal bus seating. Management then decided that irrespecive of vehicle type only the overall red treatment would be used.

The results of adoption of the 'Midland' livery and identity were that local brand names were eliminated from fleetnames, although they continued to appear on some timetable and publicity material, and Tamworth at last came into line with the rest of the fleet. As far as the latter was concerned it was accepted that the re-appearance of genuine 'Midland Red' in central Birmingham would have no downside whatsoever.

There has been implied criticism, naturally, that the change to the 'Midland Red' livery was a retrograde step, or what in certain political doctrines would be described as 'revisionist'. Arguably the most effective response which can be offered is that favourable comment has come from those who really matter, viz. the customers and the staff, rather than from marketing and design professionals.

---

21 'National Bus Company 1968-1989', p 611 *et seq.* (Transport Publishing Company, Glossop 1990)

22 Much of this discussion on the events preceding privatisation and afterwards is based upon material supplied by Charles Roberts who was with Midland Red North at Cannock at the time in question. Particular thanks are due to him for his assistance, including access to drawings and photographs.

A selection of timetables from NBC (above) and Midland Red North Ltd, showing the use of local branding.

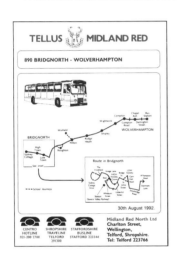

Above: Parked at Hanley bus station are two Leyland Tiger members of the 'Chaserider' coaching unit; 1518 on the left was a Duple 340 bodied example of 1986 whilst 1506 on the right was one of eight with Plaxton Paramount body new in 1983- 84. Both of these coaches were sold in April 1987.

Left: When the white/red livery became standard in 1988 a new style of destination display was introduced. The traditional style of blind with white lettering on a black ground (or black on yellow for express or trunk route destinations) was changed to white on a blue ground. The clarity was excellent, when the equipment was new but deterioration was no better than with white on black. Recently 'dayglo' fluorescent yellow on black has been introduced.

Below right: One of the Leyland Olympians which came to MRN from the Crewe- based operation of Crosville Motor Services was B 198 DTU. It became MRN 1915 and migrated to Tamworth where it is seen, still in 'Tamworth' yellow/red livery, in the summer of 1994.

Below: The yellow/red Drawlane livery was applied by Southend Transport workshops to coach-seated Leyland Olympian/ECW 1913 as the first example of this treatment of a double decker. Only the stag-head device transfer seems to have been available at the time, there being neither fleetnames nor fleet number. 1913 had operated hitherto from Cannock but after this repaint it was destined for Tamworth.

Above: The fleetname style introduced after privatisation on what became the standard white/red scheme.

Left: 968, formerly 768, (BVP 768 V) was a first in two ways. It was the first standard Leyland National to have its heating pod removed and it was also the first bus to be allocated to Stafford in the white/red livery scheme. Note that it carries only the 'Chaserider' identity at the time before the Drawlane management decided to revive reference to Midland Red. It is seen at the Rickerscote terminus in Stafford.

Lower left: Long after Cannock and Stafford had forsaken the yellow/ red livery some of Shrewsbury's minibuses could still be seen in that scheme in 1994, as shown with Ford Transit /Dormobile 96.

Below: 1703 (TPC 103 X) glows in the summer sunshine at an open day at Cannock garage in 1992. This was one of the first repaints into traditional Midland Red livery, even to the black roof on this dual-purpose example.

Gordon Weston

Above: Wellington-based Leyland Tiger with Duple Dominant bus body 1705 was selected as the first bus to wear the red 'Midland' livery. It is seen in this view fresh from the paint shops at Cannock. Note the 'Diamond Jubilee' device on the rear panel, denoting the celebration of the anniversary of the opening of Charlton Street garage.

Chapter 7

Bus Stations and Garages

Town and city termini.

As in many other parts of the United Kingdom there has been much variation in the quality of terminal points in towns and cities in the area served by MRN. Indeed, if we consider and contrast the ways in which the three county towns of Cheshire, Staffordshire and Shropshire have approached the matter we can see the whole spectrum of possibilities.

Chester was the first of the three to recognise that the time-honoured array of street stances no longer catered for the requirements of the bus-using public. Crosville received planning permission for the construction of a new bus station on the edge of the old city, whilst the city authorities themselves provided a facility closer to the shopping area; this latter development, known as the bus exchange, initially served the city's municipal bus system but has, since deregulation, provided covered platform accommodation for use by other operators.

Shrewsbury's bus terminus was for many years in a very cramped open location at Barker Street in the town centre. There were no real facilities for the travelling public, the access was poor, space for vehicles was limited and traffic movements were at times chaotic. In the late 1980s the local authority realised that a bus station should be included in the planned redevelopment of part of the town centre. This redevelopment included plans to pedestrianise a section of the Pride Hill shopping area and involved the building of the Darwin Centre shopping mall with direct access to a multi-level car park and a bus station with an enclosed passenger concourse. It is interesting to consider that in the post-deregulation era bus traffic has already outgrown the capacity of the new bus station.

In contrast the civic authorities of **Stafford**, whose predecessors had a long history of municipal vandalism, have long taken the view that the concept of a central bus station was not only unnecessary but even distasteful. Indeed at the commencement of a scheme to pedestrianise progressively the main shopping streets during the 1980s a borough official went on record to look forward to the day '...when we can get rid of the buses completely'. With the completion of the scheme, which has pushed all bus

Shrewsbury bus station is integrated with the Darwin Shopping Centre and provides covered concourse facilities for passengers with access to the buses which park nose-in at the stances.

movements to a perimeter route outside the town centre, there is little convenient access to buses for shoppers. Bus stances are scattered around the perimeter route with minimal thought for the needs of passengers who might wish to change buses. At Gaol Square there is a vestigial bus terminus equipped with two 'flow through' platforms and four less than adequate bus shelters, but even then not all services call at the facility. When a site on the edge of the town centre became vacant in 1992 it was suggested to one councillor that it would make a fine position for the long awaited central bus station; the response was that the bus companies would not pay to use it and therefore the borough council was not interested. So much for the interests of the bus travelling tax-payers and the environmentally sensible strategy of enticing people away from their cars.

Tamworth has done little better than Stafford in respect of its interest in the welfare of bus passengers. At least the street stances in Corporation Street are slightly closer to the main shopping and commercial centre of the town but covered stances are like Stafford's, totally inadequate. **Cannock** has provided a bus station, again with basic shelter for waiting passengers, but with provision for all services to use one terminating and connecting point close to the shopping centre of the town.

Wolverhampton has rationalised the vast array of bus routes of many operators into its new bus station which is situated adjacent to the railway station. This development, with enclosed 'flow-through' platforms, was jointly funded by the Metropolitan Borough Council and the West Midlands PTE. Although the bus station is some distance from the main shopping area a free shoppers' bus service operates at frequent intervals to provide a convenient means for arriving bus, and rail, passengers to reach the shops. This is perhaps one of the most imaginative developments of its kind in the country.

Macclesfield, Crewe and Oswestry have all benefited from having had in the past bus operators which built bus stations in juxtaposition to bus garages. Only in Oswestry is the combined facility rather distant from the main shopping streets of the town. Crewe's bus station is particularly well situated in this respect.

In other urban centres served by MRN, such as **Hanley** and **Newcastle-under-Lyme**, modern bus stations have been provided for use by all operators, and with advantage to bus travellers. In both cases cited the bus stations are conveniently placed with respect to the needs of the passengers. **Telford** likewise has a 'nose-in' style of bus station which is integrated with the huge central shopping centre; passengers are afforded full protection from the elements until the arrival of the appropriate bus at its departure gate, whereas nearby **Wellington** makes do with a more primitive open stance arrangeement.

Even some of the smaller centres have provided off-street facilities. **Hednesford**, **Rugeley** and **Lichfield** have all considered the advantages of having buses load and unload in central reserved areas and have acted accordingly with provision of albeit simple bus stations with stances having minimal weather protection.

The situations in Birmingham and Manchester have some common features. The central bus station in **Birmingham** was built originally by Midland Red Omnibus Company. On the split of this organisation the bus station property eventually fell under the ownership of Midland Red West who then proceeded, in the era of deregulation and privatisation, to charge other operators for the use of the facility. This action led some operators, MRN included, to use street stances for their services; indeed MRN's Birmingham services are designed to have no standing time in the city centre but merely follow a circular route through the inner city.

In **Manchester** Piccadilly bus station was built by the City of Manchester to provide a new, single bus exchange to replace a number of street termini. It then came under the control of the Greater Manchester PTA but when its executive arm, the PTE, was prepared for privatisation it returned to the control of the city. Again, as in Birmingham, the owners were obliged to charge for its use and operators looked carefully at the cost implications. MRN had the use of one stance but has no standing time facility. In consequence MRN buses serving the Macclesfield and Congleton routes followed a circular route through the city centre, in similar fashion to the Birmingham situation, calling at Piccadilly only on the inward journey.

Garages

Apart from Cannock MRN's main garage premises have been inherited from its various predecessors, Midland Red, Crosville and, indirectly, the original North Western Road Car Company. The style of these buildings reflects the philosophy of the companies in their years of growth, most dating from the 1920s and 1930s.

Shrewsbury's garage at Ditherington was opened in 1920 as a two bay unit and extended to its present four bay form in 1929. The acquisition in the early 1950s of an adjoining piece of land for use as a parking area relieved what was becoming an acute problem. Of the original BMMO premises which passed to MRN Ditherington is the oldest and is in aspect what might be thought of as the archetypal bus depot with its twin gabled faces incorporating circular louvred ventilating apertures below the apex of each of the two bays. It is capable of accommodating double-deck buses although none has been stationed there for at least twenty years.

The **Tamworth** garage premises in Aldergate comprise a four bay structure of rather plain aspect. An extension was opened in 1957 and the site cannot now be extended any further. In consequence the entrance access is rather constrained but exit is directly onto the street. There is no real provision for parking vehicles outside which is probably an advantage in times when vandalism has become endemic. As with Shrewsbury Tamworth can accommodate double-deck buses and indeed Tamworth has the largest allocation of such vehicles in the company.

Stafford had until 1992 the most modern of the former BMMO garages in MRN territory. The Pilgrim Place premises were the subject of a major reconstruction and expansion project leading to the formal opening of the new

Above: The North Walls bus terminal in Stafford is a totally inadequate affair, tolerable in fine weather as in this view, but quite uninviting in less favourable conditions.

Below: A general view of Macclesfield bus station with the garage premises behind. This style of facility was typical of many Tilling companies as was the original North Western until 1943.

Below: The concourse at Crewe bus station provides an adequate, if draughty, facility to the travelling public.

Below: The concourse at Telford bus station shows what can be done for bus passengers if the will is there.

Above left: Ditherington garage, Shrewsbury.

Above right: The five-bay frontage of Tamworth garage.

Left: Stafford garage after closing time. The congested nature of the Pilgrim Place premises is well illustrated.

Leyland Tiger 1724 receives maintenance treatment in the temporary garage premises at Silkmore Lane, Stafford.

garage in 1962. By utilising construction techniques of the period it was possible to achieve a building with a very wide span completely free from the supporting pillars which have always been a hazard to vehicle movements in older garages. For some years the allocation of double-deck buses far exceeded single deckers but since 1980 the allocation has been all single-deck.

Sadly what is believed to have been the work of an arsonist led to the total destruction of the building, and numerous vehicles, in the early hours of 2 February 1992. The decision was taken to vacate the site. Although the garage itself was modern the access was always a problem, exacerbated in recent years by the difficulty of movements from and to the increasingly busy main Newport Road. The Stafford fleet was relocated immediately after the fire at what had been one of the processing shops at the former BRC factory at Silkmore Lane to the south of the town. Although these premises are in several ways less than ideal, MRN has equipped the site with all necessary facilities with the exception of a mechanical bus washer. There is an abundance of parking area, a manned security gate with easy access to and from the town centre. Nevertheless these premises were always seen as temporary pending the construction of a new garage in the Marston Road area to the north of the town.

Wellington garage in Charlton Street was opened in 1932. In the postwar years it became increasingly obvious that those premises were quite inadequate and the decision was taken to rebuild on the same site. The result, opened in 1953, was a very stylish triple bay building with a steel framed structure and brick frontage; there is an ornamental brick pillar topped with a flagpole. Although Wellington had never had an allocation of double-deck buses it is clear that the architects were not so informed. Consequently the doorways are of sufficient height to allow double-deck buses to pass. It is of interest that in recent years there has been an allocation of two such buses, former Crosville Bristol VRTs, used mainly for schools contract work. There is a large parking area adjacent to the garage buildings [23].

The **Cannock** premises at Delta Way were designed to have the dual rôle of garage and headquarters. The facility was opened in 1977 and is of modern concept where there are 8 bays, each with an interconnected inspection pit of length to accommodate one vehicle, opening onto a very large parking area. This reflects the view that to provide covered accommodation for the fleet allocation has become much too expensive. The garage facilities are capable of carrying out all necessary maintenance and repair work, including vehicle painting. Adjacent to the main building there is a mechanical bus washer.

Connected to the garage building is a modern office block which houses the administrative heart of the company. It is a commentary on the times that by the late 1980s the operational and traffic offices for the Cannock garage itself had to be housed in a Portakabin building at the edge of the parking apron.

Crewe garage and bus station are located close to the town shopping centre. The buildings are of modern style, built by Crosville Motor Services in 1960 and reflecting the thinking of the Tilling organisation. The garage is of wide bay steel frame construction with nine bays; these are occupied by inspection pits, of sufficient length to accommodate two buses each, and a bus washing facility. The garage was designed to handle a large allocation and, with the direct access to the broad tarmac area in front of the bus station, traffic movements can be optimised.

Oswestry provides an example of a typical Crosville rural garage dating back to pre-World War 1 with an arched roof of corrugated iron on wooden beams and brick end-fill; offices and stores are located along the sides where headroom is restricted by virtue of the roof profile. There is one wide doorway which gives access to the street whilst there is an open parking area at the rear, accessed from the flow-through bus station concourse at the side of the garage building. Double-deck buses can be handled within the garage itself. The building was originally an ice skating rink.

The **Macclesfield** combined garage and bus station premises in Sunderland Street replaced inadequate premises elsewhere in the town in 1939. The design is typical of Tilling practice of the inter-war years, with the waiting room and traffic offices situated in an island building in front of the garage itself; bus movements are then catered for on a one-way circulation around the island building. The garage is a triple bay unit of conventional steel framed construction with brick infill. There is one exit door onto the bus station concourse, access being from the rear where there is a small open parking area accessed from a side street. A bus washer is sited at the rear of the garage building with the facility to drive forward into the garage if required. Double-deck buses can be accommodated.

Of the minor outstations **Congleton** and **Abermule** were established by Crosville and Crosville Wales respectively, the latter having small covered accommodation and fuelling facilities. Of the others **Bridgnorth** and **Etruria** are recent post-deregulation sites which have very little functional design for bus operation. The former, shared with Midland Red West, was originally part of a complex of redundant industrial units, with at least some facility for keeping buses under cover, although latterly both companies reverted to an open air site adjacent to the covered accommodation which was then vacated. Etruria is essentially an open area with a small office building, on a former factory site.

In November 1994 Etruria and Congleton were closed. Operations based at Etruria were transferred to the Stevensons site in Burslem with the exception of the workings on the C84 Hanley-Chester service; these diagrams with the vehicles then operated from Crewe. Congleton vehicles, by then down to four, and the associated workings were also transferred to Crewe while Macclesfield operations were transferred to Stevensons at the end of the year.

The **Woodseaves** outstation is at premises owned by Happy Days where that undertaking's own vehicles are also stabled. There is at least an established regime of bus operation at that site.

---

23 For greater detail on Midland Red garages the reader is referred to Gray, Keeley and Seale; 'Midland Red', Volume 2 (Transport Publishing Company, Glossop 1979).

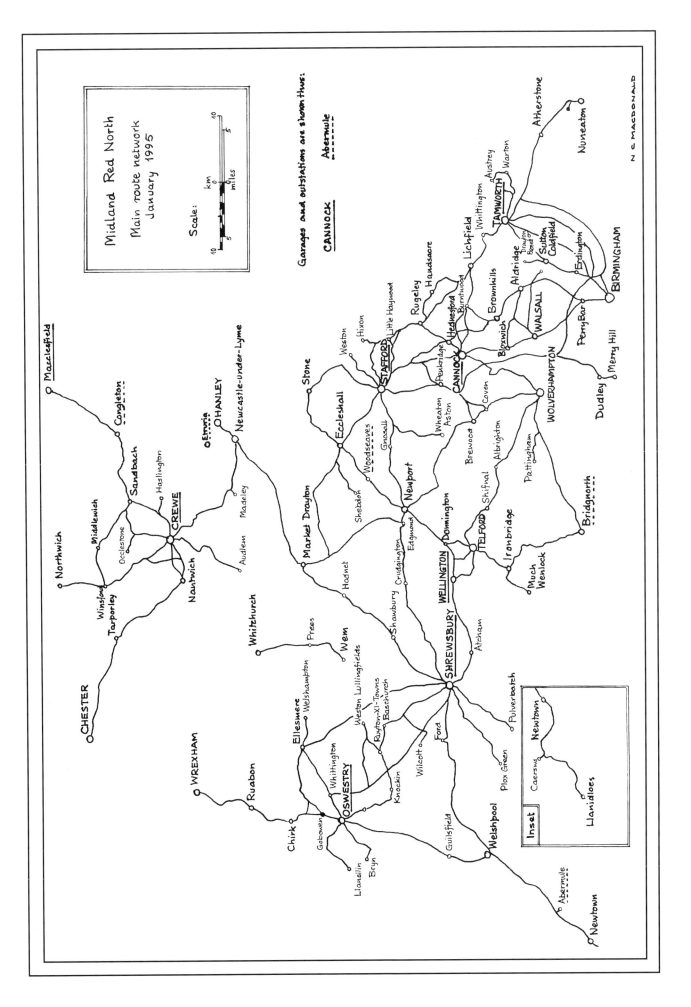

Midland Red North

Main route network
January 1995

Scale:

Garages and outstations are shown thus:

CANNOCK

Abermule

C C MACDONALD

N

Inset

49

Above left: Charlton Street garage, Wellington.
Above right: The interior of Cannock garage.

Right: A VRT, a Transit and a Dominator stand over the inspection pits at Crewe garage.

Below: A general view of Oswestry garage and, to the extreme left, the bus station with a clutch of Bristol VRTs all bar one in Crosville Wales livery.

Right: By a fortunate coincidence B 109 KPF was captured on film in Stafford in its original condition as London Country BTL9 and in Jetlink 747 livery. It is seen in Stafford's Eastgate Street.   Geoffrey Smith

Right: B 109 KPF, in its new guise as MRN 1729, with new East Lancs EL2000 body, based at the Woodseaves outstation, parks up at Tenterbanks, Stafford ready for departure on the long run to Wellington.   Geoffrey Smith

Below: A comparison of front end treatments on two EL2000 bodied Leyland Tigers. 1716 (WPH 126 Y) is one of the first batch of rebuilds of 1989 whereas newly delivered 1742 (A 42 SMA) arrived in 1991. The latter was undergoing a post-delivery check at Silkmore Lane, Stafford prior to allocation to Shrewsbury for service at Abermule.

Chapter 9

Fleet Development and the Fleet List

The beginning. Table 9.01 lists the fleet of vehicles which were transferred from Midland Red Omnibus Company Limited to the newly formed Midland Red (North) Limited on 6 September 1981. The new company, like its fellow derivatives of the old Midland Red, retained the fleet numbers which it had inherited. Indeed to the passengers there was little to indicate that any change had occurred, unless the eagle- eyed might have spotted the application of transfers on the lower nearside showing the new legal lettering. Possibly the most significant feature of Table 9.01 is that it contains no vehicles of BMMO manufacture. That there was no remnant of the once far-sighted design philosophy of Carlyle Road Works is itself adequate commentary on the rapidly changing state of the British bus industry in the late 1970s and early 1980s.

Perusal of Table 9.01 will show that the principal class of bus in the fleet was, understandably, the Leyland National of which there were 108 of the original type and 11 National 2s. The next most numerous were the Leyland Leopards with standard dual purpose bodies by Willowbrook and Marshall; there were 15 of the first combination and 26 of the second. Leyland Leopard coaches accounted for 31 vehicles, 24 with bodies by Plaxton, 6 bodied by Willowbrook and the solitary example with an Alexander Y-type body; this last vehicle, new to Stratford-upon-Avon Blue Motors, was destined to have less than a year in service before being sold for preservation.

Double-deck buses accounted for just 21 of the inheritance, all Daimler Fleetlines. Six of these had come with the Harpers business with two others ordered by Harpers but delivered new to MRN. The remaining 13 had dual-door Alexander bodies of that manufacturer's A-type to BMMO specification and classified as Midland Red type DD13, of which 103 were originally in service with Midland Red.

Finally there were 17 of the Plaxton bodied Ford R192 light weight buses which BMMO had purchased to replace their Type S14s which had dated from the mid- 1950s. The Fords, new in 1971, were never truly up to the demands placed upon them and, as a class, they were actually on the way out when the split of MROC took place. The first to go were withdrawn in early 1982 and the remainder were eliminated within twelve months.

1981-82 (Table 9.02)   lists the additions to the fleet during the first year of the newly created Midland Red North. Significantly there was no new vehicle intake but 17 Leyland Nationals, 6 Leyland Leopard dual purpose buses and 5 Plaxton bodied Leyland Leopard coaches, all originally with Midland Red, were obtained from one or other of the new companies formed at the split; curiously one of MRN's own Nationals was sold to Western National while four of the youngest Plaxton bodied Leopard coaches

went to other Midland Red companies. One Alexander bodied Daimler Fleetline, new to Trent, was also acquired; this vehicle bore more than a passing resemblance to MRN's own type DD13 Fleetlines except for its having a single door.

1983 (Table 9.03)   The significant event of 1983 was the arrival of a range of new buses and coaches, and the beginning of withdrawal of Daimler Fleetlines, although at the same time came five others including four of the ex-London Transport DMS type. Of most significance was the batch of ten ECW bodied Leyland Olympians with Gardner 6LXB engines and to National Bus Company standard specification. Along with these came six of the equally new Leyland Tiger fitted with Plaxton Paramount 50-seat coach bodies; these were equipped with Leyland's own TL11 engine.

Also on the new vehicle front came three Mercedes-Benz minicoaches for the newly introduced Rugeley Party Line venture. This was a specialist marketing innovation aimed at what was perceived as a growing opportunity in evening and weekend private hiring. There were further strange movements involving Leyland Nationals. Two more were acquired from Midland Red East whilst two of MRN's own went to Western National. Also from Midland Red East came two Midland Red type LS27 dual purpose Leyland Leopards.

Although one of the ex-BMMO type DD13 Fleetlines and two of the early Harpers Fleetlines went into retirement five other second-hand buses of the same manufacture came into the fleet. Four of these were of the London Transport DMS class, which had been with Western National, and one other of the ex-Trent Alexander bodied batch.

To complete the picture for 1983 were five Leyland Leopard coaches, all less than 18 months old. Two of these had the new ECW B51 body and it is instructive to consider whether MRN was sold a couple of pups by Southern Vectis and National Travel West. The others were truly better buys with Plaxton bodies, although in truth one of these, 1505, was technically only on loan from National Travel West for some six months.

1984 (Table 9.04)   The pattern in 1984 was in effect a continuation of what had happened the previous year with intakes of both Leyland Olympians and Tigers. The former were again bodied by ECW but this time with dual purpose 42/28 seating; they were also the first buses to be fitted with electronic destination equipment.

The Tiger purchase comprised 12 coaches, bodied by Plaxton (2) and Duple (10) to its new Laser design, plus another nine Tigers with Duple Dominant bus bodies; these were from a batch of ten, the other going to Ribble.

A further six Leyland Nationals came in from Northern General during the year while the first of the BMMO type

6434 (CHA 434 K) was one of the batch of 40 Willowbrook bodied Leyland Leopard dual-purpose buses introduced by BMMO as type LS24 in 1971. Based at Stafford it is seen at Lichfield ready for a return trip. Even in the late afternoon of a winters day the Midland Red livery with simple gold fleet names of the last style looked attractive. Note on the edge of each destination blind the code letters SD identifying Stafford as its home garage.   Gordon Weston

228 (JHA 228 L) was one of the Leyland Leopard/ Marshall dual-purpose buses from the large batch of Midland Red type LS27, new in 1973, which passed to MRN. It is heading out of Cannock for Birmingham on the X31, all steamed up on what looks to have been a truly foul day.

LS24 Willowbrook bodied Leyland Leopards were withdrawn. Further withdrawals included type DD13 and ex-Harpers Fleetlines.

An interesting initiative was the purchase of five MAN/ Göppel articulated buses with seating for 53 passengers which had been in service with South Yorkshire PTE in Sheffield. They operated from Cannock garage for some three years with some success. One disadvantage, however, was that they were too long to be accommodated within the bays of the premises at Delta Way with the doors closed.

In other respects these 6-year old vehicles were already obsolete by continental standards. The development of rear engined city buses in Germany, France and Sweden was bringing a new dimension to articulated bus design where the drive train was mounted at the rear of what had hitherto been the trailer unit; with sophisticated hydraulic linkage between the two parts of the train superior handling and manoeuvrability were claimed.

1985 (Table 9.05)   New vehicle purchases in 1985 were numerous but of an essentially different character. This was the year which saw the introduction of minibuses in Stafford and Cannock and 19 of the Ford Transit 16-seat Dormobile conversions arrived.

Also new was a midicoach, a Reeve Burgess 32-seat bodied MAN while a second-hand Plaxton bodied Bedford YMQ 30-seat midicoach joined it for the Rugeley Party Line fleet from which one of the smaller Mercedes-Benz was sold.

Only one full-size coach joined the fleet, a Plaxton Paramount bodied Leyland Tiger which had been a Leyland demonstrator. As for double-deckers, three more ex-London Transport DMS Fleetlines came from Western National while there were further withdrawals of MRN's own older examples. This was also the year which saw the elimination of the last of the BMMO type LS24 Leyland Leopards.

1986 (Table 9.06)   This was the second year of mainly minibus purchases with 40 Ford Transits and 18 Freight Rover Sherpas, all with 16-seat bodies. In all the first phase of minibus 'mania' had involved 59 Transits and 18 Freight Rover 378D vehicles, and saw minibuses now operating in Tamworth, Telford, Shrewsbury and Lichfield in addition to the 1985 introductions. Only in the last case was the venture unsuccessful with revenue failing to match operating costs and in consequence MRN discontinued minibus operations in Lichfield. The only new full-size vehicles comprised three high specification Leyland Tiger/ Duple 340 coaches and a single MCW Metroliner double-deck coach for National Express work.

Second-hand purchases included six Leopard coaches, three dating from 1976 with Plaxton bodies which came from Midland Red West and three with Willowbrook bodies new in 1982 to Midland Red Coaches.

Eight more DMS Daimler Fleetlines were acquired from Western National but at the same time the last of Midland Red's type DD13s and the remaining ex-Harpers Fleetlines were withdrawn.

1987 (Table 9.07)   The only new vehicles were 20 of the new Ford VE6 Transits with Dormobile 16-seat bodies. With deregulation opportunity had been seen in providing a minibus service in Walsall in competition with the established operator, West Midlands Travel. In the event that initiative was unable to operate profitably in face of the competitive response from the incumbent operator and upon withdrawal later in the year MRN dispersed the surplus vehicles to other garages. Nevertheless the minibuses in the heartlands of MRN territory were having real success and the minibus intake was augmented by three older Transits which came from Stevensons.

Of much more significance were the events which led to the decimation of the fleet in April 1987, discussed in detail in Chapter 3. The effect on the fleet was draconian. In what has been called in Chapter 3 'the night of the long knives' no fewer than 103 buses were withdrawn and offered for sale, including the remaining Fleetlines and a number of the recently delivered Leyland Olympians and Tigers. Certainly the introduction of newly cast urban service networks following the MAP exercise had profoundly altered the fleet requirements and had paved the way for the introduction of minibuses. The aftermath of April 1987 saw the double-deck fleet reduced to some eleven vehicles. This same slimming exercise also led to the final elimination of the once numerous dual purpose Leyland Leopards of Midland Red type LS27/28.

In all 113 buses and coaches were withdrawn for sale between February and April of that year, and are listed below.

Leyland Leopard (dual purpose): 201, 202, 210, 221, 226-229, 231, 232, 244, 246, 324, 331, 334, 338-340, 358, 359, 367, 368.

Leyland Leopard (coach): 191-193, 458, 459, 463, 467, 468, 667, 670, 681, 682, 737, 740, 792-796, 806, 1608-1610.

Leyland Tiger: 1508-1513, 1517-1520,

Leyland National: 265-268, 272, 273, 289-296, 298, 399-401, 403-405, 421, 431- 433, 483, 597, 1710, 1712, 1713, 1715, 1716.

Leyland Olympian: 1901, 1908.

Daimler Fleetline: 439, 440, 1914-1921, 1924-1928, 1930, 1932, 2234.

Others: 1, 2, 3, M2, C3, 1521.

1988 (Table 9.08)   The company was sold to Drawlane Limited on 27 January 1988 with a fleet of 248 passenger vehicles. It was inevitable that the new owners would wish to assert their presence and liveries were immediately the subject of attention as has been described in Chapter 6. At the same time the new management came to the conclusion that a change of direction was needed from that which had been the strategy of the previous management. There was a reversal of what had happened in 1987 with a very significant influx of full-size buses, mainly from other component companies of the Drawlane organisation.

Seven Leyland Nationals came from London Country (South West) including one which was never operated; another of this intake was a series B National, a type which had not hitherto been seen at any Midland Red location. In addition to these Nationals another two came from Eastern National.

Having seen the departure of a substantial tranche of its coach complement in the previous year MRN now saw the arrival of 17 Leyland Leopards variously bodied by Duple, Plaxton and ECW; these comprised 10 from North Western, new to Ribble, and 7 from the Shamrock and Rambler operation in Bournemouth. Drawlane had taken the decision to close down operation of that subsidiary because of the failure there of its crucial minibus initiative in competition with Bournemouth Transport. To complete the amazing turn-round came two MCW Metroliner double-deck coaches from Shamrock and Rambler, virtually identical to the solitary example which had been sold by MRN in 1987.

A number of 16-seat minibuses also came into the fleet from Shamrock and Rambler (9 Transits and 3 Freight Rover Sherpas) and North Western (3 Freight Rover Sherpas). Further Freight Rover/Carlyle 20-seat minibuses were acquired, three purchased and two initially as demonstrators on extended loan but finally also purchased.

Withdrawal of Leyland Nationals was continuing and curiously one of these went to London Country (South West). The withdrawal of greater significance was the complete transfer of the National 2s to North Western. It is alleged that Chris Hilditch, feeling that their Leyland L11 engines made them an anomaly, decided that he wished to concentrate upon National 1s, with the 501 engines of less than blessed reputation. A particularly useful feature of the National 2s, apart from the derivative of the well-tried 0.680 engine, was that, being without heating system pods, they could be used on the 825 Stafford-Lichfield route with its famous low bridge; having got rid of them it then became necessary to modify the heating system on some existing National 1s to eliminate their pods, thus allowing them to be available for the 825.

1989 (Table 9.09) In the first full year as a privatised company MRN's fleet was subject to a plethora of change. On the new vehicle front there came the introduction of a new type of minibus, 26 Iveco 49-10 chassis with 23-seat Carlyle bodies and four Leyland Olympians with East Lancs H45/29F bodies; the latter was a reflection of the acquisition by Drawlane of the East Lancs business from John Brown Engineering, a subsidiary of Trafalgar House.

In both the above cases it had been possible to obtain from Dudley LVLO registration marks in the xHA series, a nostalgic memory of the days when every new Midland Red bus was registered in the County Borough of Smethwick.

Minibuses were transferred in from other Drawlane companies, 16-seat Ford Transits from Midland Fox (11), 16-seat Freight Rover Sherpas from London Country (South West) (6) with Carlyle 20-seat bodied Sherpas coming from Shamrock and Rambler (2) and North Western (8). Two other Carlyle bodied Sherpas were acquired from Carlyle, formerly demonstrators.

Of major significance was the effect of the transfer of the Crewe based operations of Crosville Motor Services to MRN. This brought a total of 37 buses comprising the following;

Freight Rover minibus: 170-186;
Leyland National: 793, 794, 873, 876, 878, 890;
Leyland Leopard coach: 1301, 1302, 1304, 1308;
Leyland Olympian: 1914, 1915, 1937, 1938, 1954, 1955;
Bristol VRT: 1871, 1878, 1884, 1885.

Two more Nationals, which were new to Ribble, were received from North Western and two Leyland Leopards with Plaxton coach bodies came from the former Shamrock and Rambler fleet. Also from that source was received one other MCW Metroliner triple-axle coach to bring the number of that type to three.

Unusual newcomers were the Bristol LH6L char-à-banc conversion, ex-Shamrock and Rambler, and the return to the fleet of one of the vanished BMMO type LS24 dual-purpose Leyland Leopard/Willowbrook combination from Midland Fox. Strangely this latter bus, still with its BMMO number 6440, was destined to remain in service for another two years.

The final intake comprised 11 Leyland Tigers from London Country (South West). These came with their ECW B51 bodies, acquired by London Country for Green Line services, but in no fit state for further service. As described in detail in Chapter 8 these were given a fresh lease of life by East Lancs where new EL2000 bodies were fitted.

Withdrawals of Nationals continued in small numbers and also withdrawn were the first of the Leyland Leopard coaches, some of which had arrived only recently. This year also saw the final divorce from the MCW Metroliners.

1990 (Table 9.10) The beginnings of consolidation can be seen. The two remaining Iveco 49-10/Carlyle 23-seat minibuses of the batch ordered in 1989 arrived, with PHA registrations. New double-deckers comprised the first Dennis vehicles in the fleet, Dominators with East Lancs bodies; these reflected the favourable opinion for the marque which Geoffrey Hilditch had developed; they also had xHA registrations.

The first five of what would be the final batch of Ford VE6 Transit/Dormobile minibuses, now seating 18 passengers, arrived together with three more of the 20-seat Carlyle bodied Freight Rover Sherpas. A new type of minibus also appeared, Renault S56/Northern Counties 23-seat vehicles. Further second-hand minibuses took the form of four Carlyle bodied Sherpas from London Country (South West) but which were new to Shamrock and Rambler; Drawlane was certainly moving stock around the subsidiaries. One final minibus arrival came by a strange route from a van hire company in Exeter but via Stafford Ford dealer Lloyds.

Full-size buses came from a number of sources. Three more Leyland Nationals, this time via a dealer from Alder Valley, a dual-purpose seated version from Bee Line and a Duple bodied Leyland Tiger coach from Southend Transport completed the intake of single-deck vehicles (Managing Director Chris Hilditch had been previously with Southend).

The double-deck bus acquisitions were completed by five Bristol VRT/ECW from Bee Line but new to a variety of operators, three ex-Kelvin Scottish MCW Metrobus/Alexander vehicles and a pair of Leyland Olympian/ECW coaches; the last two had been new to Crosville Motor Services and intended for the North Wales coast express services and came from recently created Crosville Wales.

It was during 1989 that the minibus operation in Derby

Above: One of the Ford R192/Plaxton light-weight buses of BMMO type F1 makes its way toward Shrewsbury via Ludlow on the rather lengthy 435 service from Hereford.

Daniel Hill

Below: Former Harper Brothers vehicles inherited by Midland Red North were six Daimler Fleetlines. Seen here at Cannock bus station is 2233, one of a pair with ECW bodies to essentially NBC pattern new in 1973 and the only ones to have Leyland engines.

Above: Leyland National 289 (NHA 289 M) was one of the first batch of the type to arrive at Stafford. It is seen in that town in 1984.

Below: The final Midland Red version of the Leyland Leopard/Marshall dual-purpose combination was the type LS28, of which 368 was an example. It is seen in later days, in plain poppy red relieved only with the 'Chaserider' claret band and name, picking up in New Street, Birmingham on the short-lived X55 service to Cannock.   David Longbottom

was closed down; the large fleet of Freight Rover vehicles which had been drafted into Derby in 1988 and 1989 passed to the ownership of Derby City Transport in 1990 in exchange for a share in the equity of that company. In all 35 minibuses were involved.

1991 (Table 9.11) This was another year where significant change occurred. New vehicle acquisitions were mainly minibuses, completion of the 1990 orders for Renault S56/Northern Counties and Ford Transit/Dormobile types; there were also two more Freight Rover Sherpa/Carlyle vehicles.

The items of most interest were two Dennis Darts with East Lancs EL2000 style bodies. One of these was an 8.5 metre bus with 35 seats and the other a 9 metre seated for 40 passengers. They were acquired for assessment of the midibus concept and initially they were allocated for operations in the Crewe area.

Many more second-hand buses arrived. Many of these came with the acquisition of two other businesses, Happy Days and the Crosville Wales Oswestry based operations. From the former were obtained a single Ford VE6 Transit/Dormobile, a Mercedes-Benz 814D/Alexander midibus and three Scania/Plaxton buses of less than one year old; the Scanias were immediately dispatched to Wellington for Telford town service duties.

The Crosville intake was much more significant. There were three 18-seat Carlyle bodied Sherpas, two Iveco 49-10/Robin Hood 21-seaters and four similar chassis with unusual Carlyle 25-seat dual purpose bodywork. Having so recently received the first example of a B series Leyland National the Crosville Wales inheritance now provided another 12 of the type, and with them came another four Bristol VRT/ECW double-deckers. Of particular interest is that while these VRTs were arriving the company was actually getting rid of those which it had received only a year or so earlier.

The two associated Drawlane subsidiaries, Bee Line and C-Line, provided six Carlyle bodied Freight Rover Sherpas and seven Mercedes-Benz 811D with Carlyle 33-seat midibus bodies. North Western's contribution was four Renault-Dodge S46/Northern Counties 22-seat minibuses and eleven similarly bodied Renault S56 minibuses.

A most interesting purchase was the batch of six nearly new Dennis Falcons from London Country (South West). These were sent to Wellington to be assessed as ultimate replacements for Leyland Nationals, having low floor layout.

Also from London and Country, as it had now become, came four Leyland Tiger coaches, one with a Plaxton Paramount body and three Duple Lasers; the former lasted only a little over a year before being sold to the Shrewsbury independent, King Offa Travel.

Nine Leyland Tigers also came from London and Country, but not for use as received. These were 12 metre versions which had high specification bodies of either Berkhof or Duple 340 manufacture. All of these were treated in the same way as the 11 metre batch received in 1989, going to East Lancs to be re-imaged with that concern's EL2000 style body. The full story is told in Chapter 8.

Five more Tigers were given the same treatment at East Lancs. Four of these were 11 metre types, three having been ex-Green Line coaches ending up with County Bus and Coach and the other was ex-North Western with a Duple Dominant body. The fifth was a 12 metre Tiger which had been equipped with a Berkhof body and was acquired from County Bus and Coach.

Leyland Nationals and Leopards continued to be withdrawn in small numbers, the former now being scrapped whilst the latter went on to other operators. The first significant numbers of minibuses were withdrawn, some Transits being consigned to scrap whereas others as well as Freight Rovers were sold for further service. Bristol VRTs, which found no favour in the company, continued to be disposed of, mainly to Bee Line. A surprising sale was of the three Duple bodied Leyland Tiger coaches of 1984 to Grimsby-Cleethorpes Transport; these had been virtually the only high specification coaches which had survived the 1987 purge.

1992 (Table 9.12) This was a quieter year. The only new vehicles to be received were ten Dennis Falcons with East Lancs 48-seat bodies. These buses were allocated, like the earlier batch obtained almost new from London and Country, for service at Wellington. This then allowed relocation of the first batch to Oswestry where an injection of new buses was required as a condition for certain local authority tendered work.

On the minibus front new arrivals were sparse, amounting to two more Renault-Dodge S46/Northern Counties from C-Line and three Renault S56/Northern Counties, two of which were obtained from Grimsby-Cleethorpes Transport and the other from Cleveland Transit.

To complete the intake were the last three Leyland Tiger/East Lancs rebodies. Each chassis, of the 11 metre version, had a different history. Perhaps the most exotic was the one which had started out with a Duple Goldliner body as one of the Northern Scottish batch for the prestigious Aberdeen-London overnight service. One other came from County Bus and Coach as yet another of the ill-fated ECW bodied batch originally intended for Green Line duties whilst the third arrived in a dreadful state from Rhondda Transport with remnants of its original Duple coach body.

The withdrawal of the dwindling fleet of Leyland Nationals continued although this type continued to have a significant presence at Shrewsbury and Wellington. Likewise the number of Leyland Leopards was falling toward single figures in the face of the arrival of the rebodied Tigers. The older 16-seat Transit and Freight Rover minibuses also were beginning to see their numbers eroded but the most important cause of withdrawal for scrap was as a result of the fire at Stafford garage.

This disastrous event led to the loss of the following 20 buses;

      Leyland National: 956, 986, 989.
      Leyland Tiger: 1727.
      Renault S56: 342.

Ford Transit: 6, 23, 24, 81, 83, 85, 87, 89, 94, 99, 106, 108, 114, 117, 144.

1993 (Table 9.13)   This was a year with a large intake of vehicles but was the first year since 1987 without any new buses arriving in the fleet. The main reason for the influx was the integration of the C-Line operations centred on Macclesfield into MRN. These additions to the fleet numbered 47 vehicles as identified below;

Renault-Dodge S46: 360;
Mercedes-Benz 811D: 414, 431-436;
Mercedes-Benz L608D: 482-486, 497, 498;
Mercedes-Benz 709D: 490-495;
Leyland National: 825, 872, 882, 883, 890, 1056, 1067;
National Greenway: 875;
Leyland Tiger: 1618, 1639, 1660, 1698;
Leyland Olympian: 1950, 1952, 1972;
Leyland Atlantean: 2065, 2069, 2072, 2078, 2081;
Bristol VRT: 1851, 1868, 1871, 1884, 1885, 1898.

Other minibus additions comprised four Ford Transits from Midland Fox, ten further Renault-Dodge S46/Northern Counties from Bee Line and a solitary Freight Rover Sherpa from Crosville Wales. Full-size buses came by transfer from Bee Line in the form of four Leyland Olympians and four Volvo B10Ms all with Northern Counties double-deck bodies, and four Leyland Tiger buses from Timeline Travel; these latter vehicles had Alexander (Belfast) Q-type bodies which had a distinctly rugged appearance; all of these were allocated for service at Tamworth.

Withdrawals continued to follow the pattern of the previous few years, with some Leyland Nationals, Ford Transits, the odd Freight Rover Sherpa and Bristol VRTs affected; by the end of the year the Leyland Leopard had virtually disappeared, only one example remaining in service. Of the Leyland Atlanteans which came with the C-Line fleet four of these were transferred out to Bee Line during the year, leaving just one to survive until 1994; this coincided with the decision to relinquish the part of the C-Line operation based in South Manchester and in the same move the three ex-Happy Days Scanias which had been transferred to C-Line from Wellington also went to Bee Line.

1994 (Table 9.14)   In comparison with the previous year 1994 was a year of interest as far as new vehicles were concerned. Following the successful evaluation of the two Dennis Darts acquired in 1991 MRN purchased 24 of the 8.5 metre version with 33-seat East Lancs bodies; these were allocated to Cannock, Stafford and Wellington. Dudley LVLO, which would have issued the registrations, had been closed and its work transferred to Birmingham. There the LVLO had decided not to issue any xHA marks during 1994 and consequently the new buses did not carry that echo of BMMO practice. Instead they had to make do with registrations in the BNX series.

Just as there had been a swing from 16-seat minibuses to those with enhanced seating capacity, a further change of attitude was leading MRN toward midibuses as the desirable vehicles for many of its needs. Thus, following the Darts, came a batch of Mercedes 811D vehicles with

Marshall 31-seat bodies; these were similar in concept to buses operated by C-Line and recognised for their reliability, a feature noticeably absent from the Renault-Dodge S46 larger capacity minibuses which were then to be progressively displaced.

Late in the year came four further Dennis Darts of the 9.8 metre chassis type equipped with Marshall 40-seat bodies. These were for the new Shrewsbury Park and Ride contract from Meole Brace and were in the special livery specified by the local authorities.

During 1994 Stevensons came into British Bus ownership and soon afterwards some of that operator's fleet were transferred to MRN. These comprised six ageing Ford Transits and three newer Mercedes-Benz midibuses.

Eight more Leyland Tiger/Alexander (Belfast) buses came from Timeline Travel, four of which brought the Cummins L10 power unit to MRN for the first time. These were allocated to Cannock. A Plaxton bodied Tiger was obtained from Thames Transit.

Another innovation was the conversion of two Leyland Nationals by East Lancs to the Greenway design. Two more were withdrawn prior to conversion in 1995; it remained to be seen whether there would be further rejuvenations of this type.

On the withdrawal side there was further gradual erosion of the earlier Ford Transits and Leyland Nationals. The last Leopard was retired, the solitary Atlantean went to London and Country and the Bristol VRTs moved toward elimination. At last, after six years of Drawlane/British Bus ownership, some pattern was developing in terms of fleet philosophy.

The final adjustments to the fleet were concerned with the transfer on 1 January 1995 of the Macclesfield operations to Stevensons. Not all of the vehicles which were based there went with the transfer, some being retained within MRN and some others, including displaced Bristol VRTs, going to Crosville Wales; the Olympians were retained by Stevensons because of the dearth of double-deckers in that fleet, whilst the solitary Leyland National was left at Macclesfield due to its wearing a local advertising livery. The transfers are listed below;

Mercedes-Benz L608D: 483, 485, 486 (all temporarily, pending withdrawal).
Leyland National: 1067 (until the advertising contract expires).
Leyland Tiger: 1639.
Leyland Olympian: 1902, 1904, 1909, 1938, 1950, 1952.

Above: Plaxton bodied Leyland Leopard 458 sits in Ludlow, on double yellow lines, in Midland Red days. The NBC express livery with white superstructure and poppy red lower panels was certainly an improvement on the standard bus treatment. Daniel Hill

Below: 680 (SOA 680 S) was a Plaxton bodied Leopard coach new to Midland Red in 1977. It operated from Wellington for most of its life and is seen there in 'Tellus' pre-privatisation livery in 1987.

Above: Leyland National 530 is seen at Tamworth ready to take up duties on service 786 to Warton, a village to the east of Tamworth.

Berlow: An anonymous 738 (WOC 738 T), a Plaxton Supreme bodied Leyland Leopard, is seen parked up at Wellington. It wears the yellow/red Drawlane livery beside Leyland National 795 in the white/red version. The latter was one of six Nationals transferred in from London Country (South West) immediately after privatisation in 1988.

Table 9.01: Vehicles acquired by Midland Red North at formation

Fleet No.	Registration	Chassis	Body Type	New	Withdrawn	Notes
6157-6158	SHA 857-858 G	Daimler CRG6LXB Fleetline	Alexander H45/30D	1969	1986	a
6171-6173	SHA 871-873 G				1983,1986	a
6175	SHA 875 G				1983	a
6191-6193	UHA 191-193 H	Daimler CRG6LXB Fleetline	Alexander H45/30D	1970	1986	a
6201	UHA 201 H				1983	a
6216-6217	UHA 216-217 H				1986,1985	a
6274	YHA 274 J	Daimler CRG6LXB Fleetline	Alexander H45/30D	1971	1986	a
6325	YHA 325 J	Ford R192	Plaxton B45F	1971	1982	
6336-6339	YHA 336-339 J				1982	
6345	YHA 345 J				1982	
6350	YHA 350 J				1982	
6353	YHA 353 J				1982	
6367-6374	YHA 367-374 J				1982-1983	
6382	YHA 382 J				1983	
6401-6404	YHA 401-404 J	Leyland PSU3A/2R Leopard	Willowbrook DP49F	1972	1984-1985	
6408-6409	YHA 408-409 J				1984	
6412,6416	YHA 412,416 J				1984	
6420,6423	CHA 420,423 K				1984	
6430-6431	CHA 430-431 K				1984,1985	d
6434,6436	CHA 434,436 K				1984	
6442	CHA 442 K				1985	
2036	XNX 136 H	Leyland PSU3A/4R Leopard	Alexander C49F	1970	1982	b
2233-2234	TRE 948-949 L	Daimler CRL6-30 Fleetline	ECW H43/31F	1973	1984,1987	c
2229-2230	JBF 405-406 H	Daimler CRG6LX Fleetline	NCME H44/33F	1970	1983	c
2231-2232	BRE 311-312 J	Daimler CRG6LX Fleetline	NCME H44/31F	1972	1984	c
201-202	JHA 201-202 L	Leyland PSU3B/2R Leopard	Marshall DP49F	1973	1987	
207,210	JHA 207,210 L				1986	
221-222	JHA 221-222 L				1987,1986	
226-229	JHA 226-229 L				1987	
244	JHA 244 L				1987	
246-247	JHA 246-247 L				1987,1986	
249	NHA 249 M	Leyland National 1151/1R/2501	B51F	1974	1983	e
265-268	NHA 265-268 M				1987	
272-273	NHA 272-273 M				1987	f
289-291	NHA 289-291 M				1987	f
292-294	NHA 292-294 M	Leyland National 1151/1R	B51F	1974	1987	f
295	NHA 295 M		B49F		1987	
296-298	NHA 296-298 M		B51F		1987	
324,331	PHA 324,331 M	Leyland PSU3B/2R Leopard	Marshall DP49F	1975	1987	
334,338	PHA 334,338 M				1987	

Fleet No.	Registration	Chassis	Body Type	New	Withdrawn	Notes
339	SHA 639 N	Leyland PSU3B/2R Leopard	Marshall DP49F	1975	1987	
340	GJW 40 N				1987	
358-361	GOH 358-361 N				1986-1987	
367-368	GOL 367-368 N				1987	
399-401	GOL 399-401 N	Leyland National 11351/1R	B49F	1975	1987	g
402	GOL 402 N				1982	
403-405	GOL 403-405 N				1987	g
431-433	GOL 431-433 N				1987	g
439-440	JOX 439-440 P	Daimler CRG6LX Fleetline	ECW H43/31F	1976	1987	
458-459	JOX 458-459 P	Leyland PSU3C/4R Leopard	Plaxton C49F	1976	1987	f,u
460,468	JOX 460,468 P				1983,1987	f,q,u
465-467	JOX 465-467 P				1983-1987	f,u
469-470	JOX 469-470 P				1990	f,p
475-479	JOX 475-479 P	Leyland National 11351/1R	B49F	1976	1987-1989	h,v
480	JOX 480 P					
481-483	JOX 481-483 P				1987	d
497,499	JOX 497,499 P				1987,1994	h
498	JOX 498 P				1982	e
515-520	JOX 515-520 P	Leyland National 11351A/1R	B49F	1976	1987-1993	d,j,t,v,w
527-529	JOX 527-529 P				1983-1992	e,v
530	JOX 530 P				1994	
531	JOX 531 P				1990	h
536	NOE 536 R				1990,1993	h
537	NOE 537 R				1994	
538	NOE 538 R				1994	
574-575	NOE 574-575 R				1994-	v
591-597	NOE 591-597 R				1983-1991	e,h,j,m,v
598	NOE 598 R				1991	x
599-600	NOE 599-600 R				1994	
601	NOE 601 R				1987	
617-620	PUK 617-620 R		B49F	1977	1986	f
634,636	PUK 634,636 R				1986	f
635,637	PUK 635,637 R				1994	y
667,670	RDA 667,670 R	Leyland PSU3E/4R Leopard	Plaxton C49F	1977	1987	f
680	SOA 680 S				1992	
681-682	SOA 681-682 S				1987	r
683-685	TOF 683-685 S	Leyland National 11351A/1R	B49F	1977	1994	
686,689	TOF 686,689 S				1992	t
687-688	TOF 687-688 S				1994-	v
690	TOF 690 S					t
691	TOF 691 S				1993	
692-695	TOF 692-695 S				1994-	t,v
696	TOF 696 S				1994	
697-705	TOF 697-705 S					y'
717	TOF 717 S				1994	
718-719	TOF 718-719 S					t

Fleet No.	Registration	Chassis	Body Type	Year New	Withdrawn	Notes
736-741	WOC 736-741 T	Leyland PSU3E/4R Leopard	Plaxton C49F	1979	1987-1993	s,u,z
757-759	XOV 757-759 T	Leyland National 11351A/1R	B49F	1979	1986	f
763-769	BVP 763-769 V			1980		t
784	BVP 784 V	Leyland PSU3E/4R Leopard	Plaxton C53F	1980	1981	k
786-788	BVP 786-788 V				1981	m
792-796	BVP 792-796 V	Leyland PSU3E/4R Leopard	Willowbrook C53F	1980	1987	
806	BVP 806 V				1987	
807-814	BVP 807-814 V	Leyland National 2 NL116L11/1R	B49F	1980	1988	j,n
823-825	EON 823-825 V				1988	j,n

Notes

a	Sold to Ribble Motor Services.
b	New to Stratford-upon-Avon Blue Motors, passing to BMMO in 1974.　Sold subsequently for preservation.
c	ex-Harper Brothers, Heath Hayes.
d	6430, 481,482, 516, 519, 528 sold to Shamrock and Rambler Coaches.
e	249, 498, 527, 591 sold to Western National.
f	272, 291, 292, 294, 458, 459, 460, 465, 466-468, 617-620, 634, 636, 667, 670, 757-759 sold to Midland Red West.
g	399, 400, 403-405, 431-433 sold to Northumbria Motor Services.
h	477, 499, 531, 536, 595, 600 sold to London Country (South West)/London and Country.
j	515, 520, 592, 807-813, 823-825 sold to North Western Road Car Company.
k	784 sold to Midland Red East.
m	786-788 sold to Midland Red South.
n	814, 824 sold to Nottingham City Transport.
p	469, 470 later renumbered 1469, 1470.
q	460, 468 returned from Midland Red West in 1986 (see Table 9.06).
r	680 later renumbered 1480.
s	736, 738, 739, 741 later renumbered to 1436, 1438, 1439, 1441.
t	517, 686, 689, 690, 701, 768, 769 later renumbered to 917, 986, 989, 990, 901, 968, 969 when the roof pods were removed.
u	Dates of withdrawal: 1983; 460, 465, 466.
	1987; 458, 459, 467, 737, 740.
	1993; 736 (1436), 738 (1438), 739 (1439), 741 (1441).
v	Dates of withdrawal: 1983; 527, 591.
	1987; 475, 478, 515, 520, 528, 592, 597.
	1988; 477, 516, 519.
	1989; 476, 479, 593.
	1990; 594, 595.
	1991; 596.
	1992; 518.
	1994; 574, 688, 691, 693-695.
w	517 fitted with a Volvo engine.
x	Sold to Midland Fox.
y	637 converted to National Greenway by East Lancs in 1994 and renumbered 937 (see Table 9.14).
y'	704 withdrawn in December 1994 for conversion to National Greenway.
z	739 (1439) sold to King Offa Travel.

Table 9.10: Vehicles acquired during 1990

Fleet No.	Registration	Chassis	Body Type	New	Withdrawn	Notes
181-185	H 181-185 DHA	Ford Transit VE6	Dormobile B18F	1990		
218-220	H 708-710 LOL	Freight Rover Sherpa	Carlyle B20F	1990		10n
327,328	G 327,328 PHA	Iveco-Fiat 49-10	Carlyle B23F	1990		
329-332	H 329-332 DHA	Renault S56	NCME B23F	1990		
1801,1802 1803-1806	G 801,802 THA H 803-806 AHA	Dennis Dominator DDA	East Lancs H47/29F	1990		
180	F 39 HOD	Ford Transit VE6	Dormobile B20F	1988		10k
230-233	E 230-233 NFX	Freight Rover Sherpa	Carlyle B20F	1987	1994-	10e,m
859 863,866	TPE 159 S TPE 163,166 S	Leyland National 11351A/1R	B49F	1978		10f,p
874	GMB 374 T	Leyland National 11351A/1R	DP48F	1978		10d,p
1615	A 215 PEV	Leyland TRCTL11/2R Tiger	Duple C53F	1983		10g
1847	RWT 547 R	Bristol VRT/SL3/6LX	ECW H43/31F	1976	1991	10b
1851	AYG 851 S	Bristol VRT/SL3/6LXB	ECW H43/31F	1978	1991	10c
1867-1868	CJO 467-468 R	Bristol VRT/SL3/6LXB	ECW H43/31F	1977	1994,1991	10a
1890-1891	CKS 390-391 X	MCW DR102/24 Metrobus	Alexander H45/33F	1981	1993	10j
1895	ULS 615 X	MCW DR102/24 Metrobus	Alexander H45/33F	1982	1993	10j
1923-1924	B 203-204 DTU	Leyland ONLXB/1R Olympian	ECW CH42/27F	1985		10h

Notes

10a   Acquired from Glenlivet and District, Tomintoul; new to City of Oxford Motor Services; 1867 transferred to Crosville Wales, 1868 to Bee Line Buzz Company.

10b   New to West Yorkshire Road Car Company; passed to Bee Line Buzz Company.

10c   Acquired via dealer from Keighley and District; new to West Yorkshire Road Car Company; passed to Bee Line Buzz Company.

10d   Acquired from Bee Line Buzz Company; new to Crosville Motor Services .

10e   Acquired from London Country (South West); new to Shamrock and Rambler .

10f   Acquired via dealer from Alder Valley; new to Thames Valley and Aldershot Omnibus Company.

10g   Acquired from Southend Transport.

10h   Acquired from Crosville Wales; new to Crosville Motor Services.

10j   Acquired via dealer from Kelvin Central Buses; new to W Alexander and Sons (Midland); passed to Bee Line Buzz Company and onward to Midland Fox.

10k   Acquired via dealer from Panda Van Hire, Exeter.

10m   Dates of withdrawal; 1994; 230, 232, 233.

10n   Subsequently fitted with Ford engines and gearboxes.

10p   Fitted with Gardner 6HLX engines.

Table 9.11: Vehicles acquired during 1991

Fleet No.	Registration	Chassis	Body Type	Year New	Withdrawn	Notes
186-189	H 186-189 EHA	Ford Transit VE6	Dormobile B18F	1991		
191	H 191 EHA					
221	H 731 LOL	Freight Rover Sherpa	Carlyle B20F	1991		11u
229	H 729 LOL					
333	H 433 DHA	Renault S56	NCME B23F	1991		
334-339	H334-339 DHA					
501	H 501 GHA	Dennis Dart 9.8SDL3003	East Lancs B35F	1991		
701	J 701 NHA	Dennis Dart 9.8SDL3004	East Lancs B40F	1991		11v
144	D 544 HNW	Ford Transit VE6	Carlyle B16F	1986	1992	11h
241-243	D 111-113 WCC	Freight Rover Sherpa	Carlyle B18F	1986	1992	11p
245,261	D 245,261 OOJ	Freight Rover Sherpa	Carlyle B18F	1987	1993,1992	11m
251	D 111 NON					
255,258	D 155,158 NON		Carlyle B20F		1994	
276	D 176 NON				1994	
275,296	D 275,276 CEY	Iveco 49-10	Robin Hood B21F	1986		11p
283-286	F 483-486 EJC	Iveco 49-10	Carlyle DP25F	1987		11p
340-341	E 90-91 WCM	Renault S56	NCME B23F	1988		11k
343-349	E 93-99 WCM					
350	E 611 LFV					
342	E 92 WCM				1992	
351-352	D 401-402 NNA	Renault-Dodge S46	NCME B22F	1988		11k
353,354	D 448,432 NNA					
400	G 150 GOL	Iveco 49-10	Carlyle B25F	1990		11f
411,415	G 111,115 TND	Mercedes-Benz 811D	Carlyle B33F	1990		11n
421-422	G 121-122 TJA					
426-428	G 126-128 TJA					
448	F 148 USX	Mercedes-Benz 811D	Alexander DP33F	1988		11h
891-892	KMA 401-402 T	Leyland National 11351A/1R	B49F	1979		11n,w
1041-1042	EMB 641-642 S	Leyland National 10351B/1R	B44F	1978	1994-	11p,t
1052,1062	GMB 652,662 T			1979	1994	
1059,1066	HMA 559,566 T			1979		
1070	HMA 570 T			1979		
1079	ODM 679 V			1979	1994	
1080,1087	JTU 580,587 T			1979	1994	11p,t,y
1095-1096	JTU 595-596 T			1979	1994-	11p,t
1110-1112	G 610-612 CFA	Scania K93CRB	Plaxton B57F	1990	1993	11h,j

Fleet No.	Registration	Chassis	Body Type	New	Withdrawn	Notes
1201	G 301 DPA	Dennis Falcon HC	East Lancs B48F	1990		11a
1206-1210	G 306-310 DPA					
1501	A 101 JJT	Leyland TRCTL11/3R Tiger	Plaxton C57F	1983	1992	11a,r
1522	BPR 102 Y	Leyland TRCTL11/3R Tiger	Duple C50F	1983		11a
1526-1527	BPR 106-107					
1721	C 141 SPB	Leyland TRCTL11/3RH Tiger	East Lancs B61F	1986		11a,b
1722-1725	B 102-105 KPF			1984		11a,b
1726	C 262 SPC			1986		11a,b
1727	B 107 KPF			1984	1992	11a,c
1728-1729	B 108-109 KPF			1984		11a,b
1730	YPJ 207 Y	Leyland TRCTL11/3RH Tiger	East Lancs B61F	1983		11d
1737	UJN 430 Y	Leyland TRCTL11/2R Tiger	East Lancs B55F	1982		11e,s
1738	WPH 118 Y			1983		11e
1743	WPH 123 Y			1983		11e
1742	A 42 SMA	Leyland TRCTL11/2R Tiger	East Lancs B55F	1984		11g
1815,1819	YMB 515,519 W	Bristol VRT/SL3/6LXB	ECW H43/31F	1981	1994	11n,t,x
1820,1823	BMA 520,523 W				1994-	11t

Notes

11a	Acquired from London Country (South West).
11b	Originally fitted with Berkhof coach bodies which were removed by MRN and replaced with new East Lancs 2000 bodies shown.
11c	Treated as described in 11b above; destroyed by fire at Stafford garage before actually entering service.
11d	Acquired from County Bus and Coach with a Berkhof coach body; the new East Lancs 2000 body was fitted before entry into service with MRN.
11e	Acquired from County Bus and Coach; the original ECW C49F bodies were removed by MRN and replaced with new East Lancs 2000 bodies.
11f	Acquired from Carlyle Group.
11g	Acquired from North Western Road Car Company, new to Crosville; the existing Duple coach body was removed and the new East Lancs 2000 body fitted before entry into service.
11h	Acquired from Happy Days (Woodseaves).
11j	Passed to Bee Line Buzz Company.
11k	Acquired from North Western Road Car Company.
11m	Acquired from Bee Line Buzz Company.
11n	Acquired from C-Line.
11p	Acquired from Crosville Wales.
11r	Sold to King Offa.
11s	Originally registered WPH 124 Y.
11t	Dates of withdrawal: 1994; 1042, 1052, 1079, 1080, 1087, 1095, 1815, 1819.
11u	Subsequently fitted with Ford engines and gearboxes.
11v	To be renumbered 801 in 1995.
11w	Fitted with Gardner 6HLX engines.
11x	1819 transferred to Crosville Wales.
11y	1087 transferred to Clydeside 2000.

Table 9.12: Vehicles acquired during 1992

Fleet No.	Registration	Chassis	Body Type	Year New	Withdrawn	Notes
1211-1219	K 211219 UHA	Dennis Falcon HC6LXCT	East Lancs B48F	1992		
259,260	D 219,230 OOJ	Freight Rover Sherpa	Carlyle B18F	1986	1994-	12g
261	D 137 NON				1994	
355,356	D 420,436 NNA	Renault-Dodge S46	NCME B22F	1986		12e
359,362	D 319,322 DEF	Renault S56	NCME B19F	1986		12c
360	E 110 JPL	Renault S56	NCME B23F	1987		12e
365	E 325 JVN	Renault S56	NCME B19F	1987		12d
1733	LTS 93 X	Leyland TRCTL11/2R Tiger	East Lancs B55F	1982		12b
1735	DJN 25 X	Leyland TRCTL11/2R Tiger	East Lancs B55F	1982		12a
1740	AAX 590 A	Leyland TRCTL11/3R Tiger	East Lancs B62F	1983		12f

Notes

12a Acquired from County Bus and Coach; the original ECW C49F body was removed by MRN and the new East Lancs 2000 body was fitted but 1735 was used in the as-received state for some weeks; originally registered TPC 106 X, then OIB 3510; new to London Country Bus Services.

12b Acquired from Tame Valley in cannibalised condition; new to Northern Scottish with a Duple Goldliner C46FT body and registration VSS 1 X.   A new East Lancs 2000 body was fitted after extensive chassis refurbishment.

12c Acquired from Grimsby-Cleethorpes Transport.

12d Acquired from Cleveland Transit.

12e Acquired from C-Line.

12f Acquired in cannibalised condition from Rhondda Transport; the remnants of the original Duple C49FT body were removed and the new East Lancs 2000 body fitted; the original registration was A 217 VWO.

12g Acquired from King Offa Travel.   260 withdrawn in 1994.

Table 9.13: Vehicles acquired during 1993

Fleet No.	Registration	Chassis	Body Type	Year New	Withdrawn	Notes
251	E 151 AJC	Freight Rover Sherpa	Carlyle B20F	1988		13g
360	E 110 JPL	Renault-Dodge S46	NCME B22F	1987		13b
357,358	D 430,438 NNA	Renault-Dodge S46	NCME B22F	1986		13a
361,363	D 422,450 NNA					
364,366	D 423,429 NNA					
367,368	D 434,440 NNA					
369,370	D 441,444 NNA					
414	G 114 TND	Mercedes Benz 811D	Carlyle B33F	1990		13b
431-436	H 131-136 CDB	Mercedes Benz 811D	LHE B31F	1990		13b
482,484	D 202,204 SKD	Mercedes Benz L608D	Reeve Burgess DP19	1986	1994	13b,m
483	D 203 SKD				1994	13b,m,u
485,486	D 205,206 SKD				1994	13b,m,u

Fleet No.	Registration	Chassis	Body Type	Year New	Withdrawn	Notes
490	F 700 LCA	Mercedes-Benz 709D	Reeve Burgess B25F	1988		13b,n
491-492	F 701-702 KMA				1994	13b,p,u
493,495	F 703,705 KFM					13b,p
494	F 704 KFM				1994	13b,p,u
497-498	C 707-708 JMB	Mercedes-Benz L608D	Reeve Burgess B20F	1985	1994	13b,p
825	NTC 625 M	Leyland National 1151/1R	B49F	1973	1994	13b,e,w
872	GMB 372 T	Leyland National 11351A/1R		1978		13b,e,p
882,883	GMB 392,383 T	Leyland National 11351A/1R		1978	1994-	13b,d,e,p
890	GMB 390 T	Leyland National 11351A/1R		1978		13b,e,p
875	LFR 875 X	Leyland National 2 Greenway	East Lancs B41F	1981/1992		13b,s
1056,1067	GMB 666,667 T	Leyland National 10351B/1R	B44F	1978	1994-	13b,f,p
1618,1639	A 118,139 EPA	Leyland TRCTL11/2R Tiger	Plaxton C53F	1983,1984	1994-	13b,f,t
1698	A 898 KAH			1983		13b,v
1660	A 160 EPA	Leyland TRCTL11/2R Tiger	Plaxton C50FT	1983		13b,t
1745-1748	E 25-28 UNE	Leyland TRBTL11/3ARZA Tiger	Alexander B53F	1988		13z
1851	AYG 851 S	Bristol VRT/SL3/6LXB	ECW H43/31F	1978	1993	13b,q
1868	CJO 468 R	Bristol VRT/SL3/6LXB	ECW H43/31F	1977	1993	13b,r
1871	WTU 471 W	Bristol VRT/SL3/6LXB	ECW H43/31F	1980	1994	13b,p
1884-1885	WTU 484-485 W	Bristol VRT/SL3/6LXC	ECW H43/31F	1981	1994	13b,p
1898	JMB 398 T	Bristol VRT/SL3/501	ECW H43/31F	1979	1994	13b,p
1950,1952	A 150,152 UDM	Leyland ONLXB/1R Olympian	ECW H45/32F	1983	1994	13b,f,p
1972	A 172 VFM			1983		13b,p
2005,2007	G 505,507 SFT	Leyland ONCL10/1RZ Olympian	NCME H47/30F	1989		13x
2010-2011	G 510-511 SFT					
2044-2047	G 644-647 BPH	Volvo B10M-50	NCME H45/32F	1989		13y
2065	NNO 65 P	Leyland AN68A/1R Atlantean	ECW H43/31F	1976	1993	13b,
2069	TPU 69 R			1977	1994	13b,c
2072	TPU 72 R			1977	1994	13b,j
2078	SFV 428 P			1976	1994	13b,x
2081	PUF 131 M	Leyland AN68/1R Atlantean	Park Royal H43/30F	1974	1993	13b,k

Notes

13a   Acquired from Bee Line Buzz Company.
13b   Acquired from C-Line.
13c   Transferred to London and Country; new to Colchester Borough Council.
13d   882 transferred to Bee Line Buzz Company.
13e   Fitted with Gardner 6HLX engines.
13f   1067, 1639, 1950, 1952 to Stevensons.
13g   Acquired from Crosville Wales.
13j   New to Colchester Borough Council.
13k   Transferred to London and Country; new to Southdown Motor Services.
13m   New to North Western Road Car Company.
13n   New to Crosville Wales.
13p   New to Crosville Motor Services.

13q   New to West Yorkshire Road Car Company.
13r   New to City of Oxford Motor Services.
13s   New to Ribble Motor Services as a Leyland National 2 NL116L11/1R; re-constructed by East Lancs as a National Greenway.
13t   New to London Country Bus.
13u   Transferred to Crosville Wales.
13v   New to Eastern Counties Omnibus Company.
13w   New to Ribble Motor Services.
13x   Acquired from Bee Line Buzz Company; new to Kentish Bus and Coach.
13y   Acquired from Bee Line Buzz Company; new to London and Country.
13z   Acquired from Timeline Travel.

Table 9.14: Vehicles acquired during 1994

Fleet No.	Registration	Chassis	Body Type	Year New	Withdrawn	Notes
451-462	M 451-462 EDH	Mercedes-Benz 811D	Marshall B31F	1994		
502-504	L 502-504 BNX	Dennis Dart 9SDL3034	East Lancs B33F	1994		
505	L 605 BNX					
506-517	L 506-517 BNX					
518,520	L 618,620 BNX					
519	L519 BNX					
521-523	L521-523 BNX					
802-805	M 802-805 MOJ	Dennis Dart 9.8SDL3004	Marshall B40F	1994		14h
123,129	C 523,499 TJF	Ford Transit	Rootes B16F	1986		14c
131,137						
200	B 730 YUD	Ford Transit	Carlyle B20F	1985		14d,f
203-204	B 733-734 YUD					
202	B 875 EOM		Carlyle B20F	1985		14d
205	C 85 AUB	Ford Transit	Carlyle B18F	1986		14d,g
206	C 726 JJO	Ford Transit	Carlyle B20F	1986		14d,f
446	H 196 JVT	Mercedes- Benz 814D	Wright B33F	1990		14d
449	G 399 FSF	Mercedes-Benz 811D	PMT B33F	1990		14d
450	G 900 TJA	Mercedes-Benz 811D	Mellor B32F	1990		14d
937,952	PUK 637,652 R	Leyland National 1 Greenway	East Lancs B49F	1977/1994		14e
1642	D 442 CNR	Volvo B10M-61	Plaxton C46FT	1987	1994	14a
1749-1752	E 29-32 UNE	Leyland TRBTL11/3ARZA Tiger	Alexander B53F	1988		14b
1753-1756	F 33-36 ENF	Leyland TRBL10/3ARZA Tiger	Alexander B55F	1988		14b
1778	F 278 HOD	Leyland TRBTL11/3R Tiger	Plaxton B54F	1988		14j

Notes
14a   Acquired from Express Travel; transferred back later to Express Travel.
14b   Acquired from Timeline Travel.
14c   Acquired from Midland Fox.
14d   Acquired from Stevensons.
14e   Renumbered from 637, 652 on conversion to National Greenway.
14f   New to City of Oxford Motor Services.
14g   New to West Yorkshire Road Car Company.
14h   Acquired for Shrewsbury Park and Ride and painted in the special livery for the contract.
14j   Acquired from Thames Transit.

Leyland National 768 was new in 1980. It is seen in pre-privatisation 'Tellus' livery outside Charlton Street garage, Wellington displaying the now prevalent but inane legend 'Sorry-Not on Service'.

The first Stafford-based bus to receive the traditional red livery in 1992 was 969 (BVP 769 V). It was also one of the standard Nationals to have the heating pod removed, when it was renumbered from its original 769. By the time it was seen in Stafford in 1994 it had received a re-paint and had lost the BMMO garter from the rear panel.

796, one of three Leyland Leopards with the unloved Willowbrook 53-seat coach body, calls at Delta Way, Cannock on its way from Birmingham to Rugeley on the X31. The Midland Express livery of the 1980s is worn with 'Chaserider' identity.

Stafford was one of two MRN garages to have an allocation of Leyland National 2 vehicles. Here 814 (BVP 814 V) in the newly introduced white/red livery heads into the town centre from Manor Estate, with incorrectly set destination blind.

196, a Plaxton Supreme bodied Leyland Leopard dating from 1973, was acquired with four others of the same batch from Midland Red (Express) Limited in 1982 and was the last to survive with MRN, being withdrawn in March 1987. It is seen in Midland Express livery in Birmingham.

648, a Leyland National transferred in from Midland Red East in 1982, is seen in High Street, Shrewsbury with an unusual advertising treatment for the Pride Hill Shopping Centre.

Former London Transport DMS class Fleetline 1915 loads passengers in New Street, Birmingham. It would seem an unlikely candidate for service on express route X55 to Cannock and the curiously named Boney Hay. David Longbottom

MRN's first new double-deck buses were ten Leyland Olympian/ECW vehicles to NBC standard specification delivered in 1983. 1909 loads at Cannock during in the summer of 1984 wearing standard poppy red, 'Chaserider' local name and the double-N logo.

The 1983 Leyland Tiger/Plaxton coach allocated to Shrewsbury and the 'Hotspur' coaching unit was 1508, seen at Ditherington. AdrianPearson

Above: Leyland Tiger/Plaxton coach 1507 is prepared at Barker Street for a journey to Hanley on service X64.   Geoffrey Smith

The Rugeley Party Line unit was established in 1983 with three Mercedes/Reeve Burgess minicoaches. A 21 FVT was one of a pair based on the Mercedes-Benz L508D with fourteen seat bodies.

1503 (SLJ 386 X) was new to Hants and Dorset in 1982. It was acquired in 1983 from Shamrock and Rambler along with several other Leyland Leopard coaches from a variety of sources. It was a Plaxton-bodied example and was withdrawn in 1989 when it had received the yellow/red livery. The location is Corporation Street, Tamworth.

Above: Stafford-based 1491, a Leyland Leopard with ECW B51 coach body, arrives in Lichfield city centre on its way to Tamworth. Obviously one of the few virtues of the ECW body seen by MRN was the ability to negotiate the low bridge at Little Haywood. Originally numbered 1502 by MRN, ANA 91Y was new to National Travel West. It was withdrawn in 1990.

Daniel Hill

Coach-seated Olympian 1913 (B 913 NBF), one of three, approaches Cannock on X31 duty from Birmingham. The Midland Express livery is looking somewhat shoddy and there is evidence of paint peeling from the front upper deck panel.

Another of the trio, 1911 (B 911 NBF), is a regular on the 110 and 116 services from Tamworth to Birmingham. It is seen arriving at Tamworth with an unusually clear display on its electronic destination equipment.

Duple Laser bodied Tiger 1514 exits Tamworth garage in the 'Mercian' coach livery of the pre-privatisation era. This vehicle, new in 1984, was sold to Crosville along with its partner 1515 in 1989, passing to PMT in 1990. *Daniel Hill*

Of the sixteen Leyland Tiger coaches purchased in 1984 there were three with 57-seat Duple Laser bodywork. 1601 (A 601 HVT) was one of the trio, seen here at the Lichfield garage in the yellow/red livery style of the Drawlane era. With its two sisters it was sold to Grimsby-Cleethorpes Transport in 1991.

Driver Phil Bates turns Leyland Tiger 1516 at Pattingham Church ready for a return trip to Wolverhampton.

Duple Dominant bodied Leyland Tiger 1705 (A 705 HVT) approaches Stafford Market Square on a local service. It was one of the few buses allocated to Stafford to have the garish livery adopted by the Management Buy-Out team in the run-up to privatisation.

Bridgnorth-based Leyland Tiger/Duple Dominant 1707 makes an attractive picture in the summer sun as it approaches Wolverhampton bus station.
Gordon Weston

MAN articulated bus 1804 (DAK 304 V) seen at a rally.

One of the first series of Ford Transit 'Chaserider' minibuses sits in Stafford Market Square at the Christmas season.

A gaggle of 'Hotspur' minibuses gathers at Barker Street, Shrewsbury in the early days of operation, the buses being in the first livery style.

Geoffrey Smith

C 302 UVT was a Reeve Burgess bodied MAN minicoach for the Cannock-based Rugeley Party Line unit. It did not carry its allocated fleet number M2.

Les Simpson

The short-lived Bedford YMQ/Plaxton 30-seat coach numbered C3 in the Party Line fleet is seen at Cannock shortly before sale in 1987.

Charles Roberts

1517 was a Plaxton Paramount bodied Leyland Tiger, a former demonstrator acquired in 1985, which wore the short-lived 'Chaserider' livery prior to disposal in April 1987.　　　Charles Roberts

The first Freight Rover minibuses arrived in 1986, a batch of eighteen. Eleven subsequently went to Derby City Transport in 1990 but 65 (D 65 YRF), seen in Tamworth, was one of those disposed of through dealers.

In its endeavours to make things difficult for bus operators and passengers alike the Borough of Stafford not only pushes buses to the periphery of the shopping area but then places speed-reducing humps in their path. One such location is in Earl Street where Ford Transit 48, attractive in red livery, is seen negotiating one particularly difficult obstacle.

In 1986 MRN received a quartet of high specification Duple 340 bodied Leyland Tigers. One each received 'Chaserider', 'Hotspur', National Express 'Rapide' and 'Force Ten Leisure' liveries. 1520 is seen in this last guise, the branding used by the 'Mercian' coaching unit based at Lichfield. None of these coaches was destined to have much of a career with MRN, all falling victim to the 'night of the long knives' purge of April 1987.   Geoffrey Smith

1460, formerly 460, a Leyland Leopard with Plaxton coach body wears Midland Express 'Hotspur' livery in this 1988 scene at Shrewsbury's Barker Street terminal. It is preparing to operate through to Newport via Telford on service 82. This coach went to Midland Red West in 1983 for three years before its return to MRN.   Gordon Weston

A night study of a string of DMS Fleetlines in standard poppy red at Cannock garage.
Charles Roberts

A batch of thirty of the new Ford Transit VE6/Dormobile minibuses were delivered in 1987. Many of these were used initially for the foray into Walsall, until MRN pulled out. 99 is seen subsequently in Stafford where its tenure was to be curtailed, being destroyed in the fire at Stafford garage.

Amongst the transfers of Leyland Nationals from London Country (South West) was 895 (BPL 495 T), the first B-series example to join MRN. It is pictured standing at one of Stafford's street stances in Eastgate Street.
Geoffrey Smith

799 (WNO 564 L) was a one of two Leyland Nationals acquired from Eastern National in 1988, destined to have but two years life with MRN. It is seen leaving the stances at Telford bus station showing an unusual treatment of the rear panel.
Geoffrey Smith

A number of Leyland Leopards with Duple Dominant II coach bodies were obtained from North Western in 1988, but which were new to Ribble. At first they were decked out in the yellow/red Drawlane livery but eventually appeared in the white/red version, as seen here. 1342 (WCK 142 V) stands at Pitcher Bank, Stafford awaiting departure time to Knightley on route 432; this was one of the services which were inherited from Happy Days in 1991
Geoffrey Smith

ECW bodied Leyland Leopard coach 1492 (YEL 92 Y) was new to Hants and Dorset, but coming to MRN from Shamrock and Rambler with two others in 1988. It was withdrawn in 1990 and sold to Northern Bus Company. It is seen soon after arrival with 'Chaserider' name and the stag-head emblem in the early Drawlane yellow/red coach livery.
Gordon Weston

One of the former Shamrock and Rambler Duple bodied Tigers, 1653, manoeuvres in Shrewsbury bus station. It has acquired a novel modification to its yellow/red livery scheme, with full frontal red treatment.

Right: Shrewsbury was home to a variety of Freight Rover minibuses for a time. 150 was one of three of the 365D type which had Dormobile 16-seat bodies and having come from North Western in 1988. Most of the breed went to Derby City Transport in 1990.

Below: In 1988, shortly after the company was purchased by Drawlane, two MCW six-wheeled MCW Metroliners were transferred in from the Shamrock and Rambler subsidiary. One of these, B 117 ORU, received fleet number 1997 although there is scant evidence of that in this picture of it at a bus rally. It spent its short career with MRN (it was withdrawn in 1990) based at Tamworth and was often seen on the X76 Nuneaton-Tamworth-Birmingham service.   Daniel Hill

Opposite page:

Top left: Other Freight Rover based minibuses were acquired from various sources from 1988. 254, with 20-seat Carlyle body, came from North Western in 1989 and is seen at Cannock in a combination of the newly introduced white/red Drawlane livery and full-side advertising.

Top right: This rather shabby-looking Freight Rover 365D with Dormobile 16-seat body was 185, one of a number which came from Crosville Wales in 1989. It is seen still in a 'mongrel' livery but with 'Midland Red Line' fleet names. It went to Derby City Transport in 1990.   Geoffrey Smith

This page:

Top left: The Carlyle minibus conversion on Ford Transit D 202 FFX was originally one of the Shamrock and Rambler vehicles which attempted to wrest traffic away from Bournemouth's transport undertaking after deregulation. When that venture failed the buses were dispersed to other Drawlane companies and MRN fell heir to nine of these vehicles. The scene is Corporation Street, Tamworth and the bus shown has MRN fleet number 112.

Left: The rear view of the Iveco 49-10/Carlyle combination is well illustrated by newly delivered 304 (F 604 EHA). 12 of the batch of 26 delivered in 1989 went to Shrewsbury together with two similar vehicles a year later.

Below: One of Shrewsbury's large allocation of Carlyle bodied Iveco 49-10 minibuses, 307, at Shrewsbury bus station.

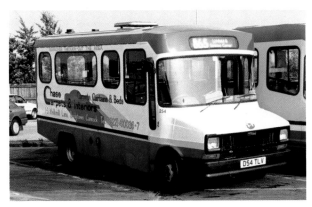

Below: An unusual purchase in 1989 was the small batch of four Leyland Olympians with East Lancs bodies. Three were allocated to Tamworth, including 1916 seen here in Corporation Street, whilst the fourth went to the newly acquired garage at Crewe.

Above: Bristol VRT 1878 is seen about to leave Macclesfield on a local town route. It wears a fairly smart dark green/cream C-Line livery which must have been one of the last to be applied. This bus was not one of the C-Line vehicles taken under MRN management but was transferred from Oswestry before the decision was made to adopt the red 'Midland' livery for the C-Line operating area. At the end of 1994 it was destined to return to Crosville Wales when the Macclesfield operations were handed over to Stevensons.

Left: Bristol VRT 1835 leads a string of four such buses assembled at Crewe Station on a British Rail replacement duty. The rear two are PMT owned, unlike the MRN examples still with their original owners.

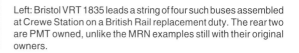

Crewe-based Olympian 1937, one of the ex-Crosville specimens, arrives in Chester on service C84 from Hanley.

Geoffrey Smith

Amongst the number of Leyland National imports was 796 (UHG 758R), one of two which came from North Western in 1989 but new to Ribble. The location is New Street, Birmingham.

Gordon Weston

Plaxton bodied Leyland Leopard 1426, carrying cherished registration HKP 126, was new to Hants and Dorset as APR 818 T, passing to Shamrock and Rambler and thence to MRN. It loads at Stafford Market Place on a town service. Gordon Weston

Midland Red North 1 (TR 6147) is not what it appears. It is in fact a Bristol LHL chassis with a reproduction char-à-banc body built by Hants and Dorset in 1983. Originally it had an ECW 43-seat bus body with registration NLJ 516 M. In its present guise it passed to Shamrock and Rambler and from there within the Drawlane empire to MRN.

Gordon Weston

An interesting introduction during 1994 was the extension of service 825 from its Tamworth terminus to the theme park at Drayton Manor Park. Stafford-based 1712 (TPC 102 X), one of the Leyland Tigers rebodied by East Lancs, picks up passengers at the park entrance for the return trip to Stafford.

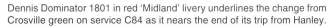

Dennis Dominator 1801 in red 'Midland' livery underlines the change from Crosville green on service C84 as it nears the end of its trip from Hanley.

Dennis Dominator 1802, in white/red livery, leaves Crewe on its way to Hanley via Newcastle.

Red-liveried second generation Ford Transit minibuses can look quite attractive especially in bright sunlight, as here with 184 at Gaol Square, Stafford.

183, one of MRN's last purchase of Ford Transit/ Dormobile minibuses, is seen at Crewe bus station.
Geoffrey Smith

Leyland National 866 (TPE 166 S) sits at its stance at Telford bus station, operating on one of the town services. This was one of the incomers from Alder Valley in 1990.
Geoffrey Smith

MRN and PMT operate the X64 Shrewsbury-Hanley service jointly, with one bus from each operator involved on the essentially two-hourly frequency. Market Drayton is the half-way point and in normal circumstances the two buses pass there. MRN 1615 (A 215 PEV), a Duple bodied Leyland Tiger obtained from Southend Transport in 1990, is a Shrewsbury-based vehicle and is loading at Market Drayton on its way to Hanley. It is a pity that the bus has a somewhat decrepit appearance, with even the 'Hotspur' identity too ashamed to show itself.

MRN acquired three MCW Metrobus vehicles with Alexander bodies from Kelvin Scottish in 1990, of which the third, 1895, is seen at Crewe. All three had been transferred to Bee Line in 1993.   Geoffrey Smith

1923 was one of two Leyland Olympian double deckers acquired with the Crosville Wales Oswestry base in 1990. They had ECW coach-seated bodies and were intended for the Crosville routes along the North Wales coast. It was allocated to Tamworth where it is seen in yellow/red livery. This bus carries the name Geoff Thompson in memory of a former driver who was held in great esteem at Tamworth.

331, one of Tamworth's Renault S56/Northern Counties 23-seat minibuses looks attractive in its gold-lined red livery. It is operating on a route to Dordon, on the edge of the Tamworth conurbation.

Dennis Dart 501 was one of the two evaluation vehicles, new in 1991. After its spell based at Crewe it was transferred to Wellington in 1994, where it is seen freshly painted in the 'Midland' livery.

Dennis Dart 501 in its days with 'Midland Red Line' branding is seen on a service to Etruria, a district of Stoke-on-Trent.   Geoffrey Smith

After extensive evaluation at Crewe Dennis Dart 701 was transferred to Stafford where it is seen after a washdown at Silkmore Lane.

JTU 580 T was one of the Crosville Wales vehicles transferred to MRN in 1991. It was one of twelve similar series B Leyland Nationals, new to Crosville which came with the operations at Oswestry. Numbered 1080 by MRN it is seen at Shrewsbury bus station, still in the colours of its former owners but with 'Cambrian Midland Red' identity and the inevitable 'Alfred/Rudolph' on the front dash panel.
Geoffrey Smith

One of the five buses which came to MRN with the stage carriage business of Happy Days (Woodseaves) was this Alexander bodied Mercedes-Benz 814D midibus. It has dual-purpose seating and is used mainly on country routes. On the occasion of the photograph, however, 448 was operating on a Stafford town service.

One of the three ex-Happy Days Scania/Plaxton buses, 1112 (G 612 CFA), pulls away from Telford bus station on town service 12 to Woodside and Madeley. All three of these vehicles were put to work in Telford when they were acquired but were transferred to the Macclesfield-based C-Line operation when that came under MRN control. By 1993 they had moved again, this time to associate company Bee Line. Note in the left background the former Trent Leopard ACH 308 B with BET standard Marshall body dating from 1964.   Geoffrey Smith

One of the Leyland National B-series buses acquired from Crosville Wales with the Oswestry operations in 1991 was 1059 (HMA 559 T), seen at Stafford's best, but still primitive, attempt at a bus station at North Walls.

1820, a Bristol VRT, came from Crosville Wales into the MRN fleet. It was later transferred to Crewe but not before it had been lettered 'Cambrian Midland Red'. Still in its former operator's livery it has lost the 'Cambrian' but without replacement.

Another of the ex-Crosville Wales Bristol VRTs, 1823, approaches Shrewsbury bus station on an inward run from Oswestry, the driver having already changed the destination display for the return trip.

Shrewsbury inherited two Iveco 49-10/Robin Hood 21-seat minibuses from Crosville Wales in 1991. 275 (D 275 CEY) reverses into a parking slot at Shrewsbury bus station.

258 (D 158 N0N), a Freight Rover Sherpa with 18-seat Carlyle body, was on loan from Oswestry in the weeks following the Stafford fire. It still wears the 'Cambrian Midland Red' fleetname. This was one of six similar vehicles which came to MRN from Bee Line Buzz Company. The Birmingham registrations indicate that they were registered by Carlyle when new. Like most of this type it was sold by MRN by 1994.
Geoffrey Smith

Mercedes-Benz 811D/Carlyle 411 was acquired with six others from C-Line in 1991. They work out of Crewe where 411 is seen entering the bus station. Geoffrey Smith

Ex-Bee Line Renault-Dodge S46, 352, was one of the first of the type with MRN, arriving in 1991. It stands at a stance in Earl Street, Stafford

Former North Western Renault S56/NCME minibus 343 on Tamworth town service 2 in Corporation Street.

A Le Mans style start at Hednesford bus station sees 415, an Alexander bodied Mercedes-Benz 811D ex-C-Line, and 766, one of the final delivery of Leyland Nationals to Midland Red, in apparent contention. At the time of this photograph 415 was a recent transfer from Congleton and still carries 'Midland Red Line' notation.

G 150 GOL was on extended loan from Carlyle Group for a time in 1991, being subsequently purchased by Midland Red North and given the fleet number 400. It is an Iveco 49-10 with Carlyle 25-seat body and is at Telford bus station.
Geoffrey Smith

A 101 JJT was acquired from London and Country in 1991, having arrived there from Shamrock and Rambler. A Leyland Tiger with Plaxton Paramount body, it was numbered 1501 by MRN and allocated to Wellington where it is seen here. Surprisingly, in view of the large intake of Tigers at that time, 1501 was sold the following year to local independent King Offa Travel Services.

Oswestry-based Dennis Falcon 1206, originally with London and Country, prepares to leave Welshpool on the scenic route D71 back to its home.

1527, a Duple Laser bodied Leyland Tiger of 1983, waits for time at Newport High Street on its way to Wellington from Stafford. This vehicle, with two others of the same batch, came to MRN in 1991 from London and Country but were originally with Shamrock and Rambler. 1527 and sister 1522 were based at the Woodseaves outstation whilst the third of the trio, 1526, was at Stafford.

Although most of their time is spent on interurban routes the East Lancs bodied Leyland Tigers can be seen on more prosaic duties. 1723 (B 103 KPF), in red with black roof, is seen on such an occasion in Wolverhampton Road, Stafford. MRN decided to discontinue the use of the former Midland Red dual-purpose livery style after it was applied out of character to 1723, a vehicle with bus seating.

Abermule-based 1737 arrives in Welshpool from Llanidloes on its way to Shrewsbury. It carries 'Cambrian Midland Red' livery and registration UJN 430 Y; its original, however, was WPH 124 Y indicating its beginnings as one of the Green Line batch for London Country.

MRN purchased a batch of ten Dennis Falcons with East Lancs EL2000 bodies in 1992. All were allocated to Wellington. A regular duty for these vehicles is the 892 service from Wellington and Telford to Wolverhampton, on which 1215 is seen entering Queen's Square near the end of its journey. These buses were the last to be outshopped in the white/red livery. They were also the only EL2000 bodied buses to have dot matrix destination displays, and the inadequacy of these is apparent.

Ready to leave Tamworth for its return journey to Stafford in the hands of Driver Dave Bell is East Lancs bodied Leyland Tiger 1733 (LTS 93 X). This was one of the last of the renovations carried out by MRN, in this case the original body being a Duple Goldliner. In that form the vehicle was new to Scottish Bus Group company Northern Scottish for the Aberdeen-London service and carrying registration VSS 1 X.

1219 (K 219 UHA) was the first of the 1992 Dennis Falcons to receive the 'Midland' livery. At the same time it was relocated from Wellington to Shrewsbury and in the process it lost its dot matrix electronic destination equipment in favour of 'dayglo' blinds. It is leaving the bus station on town service 1 to Abbots Green.

Above: With the transfer of C-Line operations to MRN came a number of Mercedes-Benz L608D midibuses, including 486, one of five which were new in 1986 to North Western. It has a Reeve Burgess dual-purpose 19-seat body, seen in Macclesfield still in C-Line livery.

Above: MRN 492, a Mercedes-Benz/Reeve Burgess midibus, still wears a rather weather-worn C-Line livery when seen at Macclesfield in 1994. It was new to Crosville in 1988.

Left: Freshly painted 493, one of the newer Mercedes-Benz 709D midibuses received with the C-Line operations, stands inside Macclesfield garage.

Below: 497 was one of Crosville's Mercedes-Benz L608D/ Reeve Burgess midibuses, new in 1985 and coming to MRN via C-Line.

The first National Greenway in the MRN fleet, 875, came with the C-Line operation. Originally a Ribble National 2 it is seen at Macclesfield in 1994; it stayed with MRN after the transfer of Macclesfield garage to Stevensons.

Above: Series B Leyland National 1067, new to Crosville, looks particularly unattractive in an all-over white advertising livery. It is seen leaving Macclesfield bus station.

Above right: The Plaxton bodied Tigers ex-C-Line have been the regular performers on the Macclesfield-Crewe service 38. 1639, new to London Country, departs from Macclesfield on its way to Crewe. This was the only one of the four such vehicles to be transferred to Stevensons on 1 January 1995.

Right: Leyland Tiger/Plaxton coach 1660 stands in the parking yard behind the Macclesfield premises.

An attractive setting in Handforth shows ex-Crosville Leyland Olympian/ECW 1952 (A 152 UDM) returning to Macclesfield from Manchester on the trunk route 130. This was one of six Olympians which passed to Stevensons with the Macclesfield operations on 1 January 1995.

251 was a Freight Rover Sherpa with Carlyle 20-seat body which came from Crosville Wales in 1993. It was allocated to Cannock where it is seen on a local route serving Pye Green and Hednesford.

Of the batch of Renault-Dodge S46/Northern Counties minibuses acquired from Bee Line in 1993 five went to Crewe, where 369 is captured on a town service departure.

2007 (G 507 SFT) was one of four Leyland Olympians with Northern Counties bodies which came to MRN in late 1993 from Bee Line. These buses were new to Kentish Bus, a subsidiary of Proudmutual, hence the registrations issued by Newcastle-upon-Tyne LVLO. All four were allocated to Tamworth for use on the well used commuter routes into Birmingham.

Carr's Lane, Birmingham is the location where Tamworth-based 2044, a Volvo B10M-50/Northern Counties, new to London and Country, loads for its return trip.

The first batch of Leyland Tiger buses acquired from Timeline Travel in 1994 went to Tamworth. Their main area of operation is on the trunk services to Birmingham, although occasionally they fulfill Tamworth's only contribution to the Stafford service, the single X25 roster. 1748 is seen at its home base on a Birmingham duty. The uncompromising lines of the Alexander (Belfast) body have led to the nickname 'Bosnian tanks'.

One of the Dennis Darts, 517, pulls away from the North Walls terminal, Stafford on a town service. These midibuses were allocated to Cannock, Stafford and Wellington.

A three-quarter rear view of Dennis Dart 514 showing the neat appearance of the East Lancs EL2000 design on the midibus chassis.

Midland Red North purchases of 1994 included a batch of Marshall bodied Mercedes-Benz 811D midibuses. One of Stafford's allocation, 454, pulls away from the North Walls terminal on one of the Eccleshall corridor services.

November 1994 saw the introduction of a new Park and Ride scheme in Shrewsbury with MRN as the successful candidate. Four Dennis Darts with Marshall bodies entered service dressed in the special livery specified by the local authorities. 805 approaches a town centre stopping place in High Street.

Left: 207 was one of four Carlyle bodied Ford Transit minibuses acquired in 1994 from the associated Stevensons operation. These had been new to City of Oxford in 1985. It was allocated to Cannock and is seen on local service work at Hednesford.

Below left: Former Timeline Leyland Tiger 1754, one of the second set acquired, climbs toward Bednall Head on a fine autumn day, operating on the 838 Stafford-Cannock service. The Alexander (Belfast) Q-type body presents a rugged but functional appearance.

Below right: 937 and 952 were rebuilt by East Lancs as Greenways from the former 637 and 652 Nationals late in 1994. Both were allocated to Shrewsbury where 937 is seen in High Street on a local town service in the first month of service.

Chapter 10

Miscellany

ANCILLARIES

Some of the more interesting features of the history of a bus company relate to peripheral matters. With that in mind this chapter addresses a range of miscellaneous subjects, mostly by illustration. Ancillary vehicles, such as driver trainers and recovery vehicles, or wreckers as they are known within MRN, have an appeal of their own. Demonstrators and loaned buses bring a transient novelty to normal operations and may provide clues to management thinking for future action. Likewise the fate of buses sold on for further service always has an air of nostalgia, unless the type involved has had a poor operational history with its former owners.

The above subjects have been dealt with on an essentially *ad hoc* basis. Indeed the coverage has reflected the availability of interesting photographs. The section on competitors and friends, however, has been put together as an attempt to portray the current atmosphere in the bus industry engendered by the climate of deregulation and privatisation. In spite of the coalescence of many companies into the new larger groups there is still much variety to be seen in most areas of the country and the pictures have been chosen to give a flavour of how the situation impacts upon MRN's operations without attempting to be an exhaustive coverage. If the reader's favourite MRN competitor has been omitted that is no reflection upon it, rather it reflects a constraint of available space.

Leyland PD2A Titan GRY 50 D, new to Leicester City Transport, came from Shamrock and Rambler and was used as a driver trainer from 1989 until 1993 when it was sold. It is seen at Delta Way in a special version of the white/red Drawlane livery. Note that coach-seated Olympian/ECW 1913 still carries Midland Express livery although by the time the photograph was taken that consortium would have been disbanded.

Cannock's ERF recovery vehicle cuts a fine line in the autumn sunshine with Dave Tew in command.

Stafford acquired this well turned out tow wagon from Cannock. It looks well in the red 'Midland' livery, still showing more than a trace of its origins as a Midland Red type LC9 coach.

Wellington's tow-wagon SBF 233 is derived from an ex-Harpers Leyland Titan. In its bus days it had carried a Northern Counties body and eventually received Midland Red fleet number 2225, which it still wears. The Titan is of type PD2A/28 and is the only example of that type built by Leyland. It looks particularly attractive in a yellow/white/red version of 'Tellus' livery, thanks to the attention of John Davis.

DEMONSTRATIONS AND BORROWINGS

G 654 EVN was an Omni demonstrator from CVE which spent a short time on assessment at Cannock. In spite of its unusual low floor design its sojourn with MRN did not lead to any orders.

A Mercedes-Benz based Optare demonstrator midibus was on loan for a few weeks in 1991. Part of its time was spent at Shrewsbury where it is seen parked at Ditherington garage. Again no orders followed.

Rossendale Transport lent their East Lancs bodied Leyland Tiger 93 (F 93 XBV) for evaluation and proving trials before the order for rebodying of the ex-London and Country Tigers was confirmed.

Plaxton 'Citybus' bodied Leyland Tiger, C 359 VUM, was at Cannock for demonstration purposes. No orders emerged although the body design arrived at MRN in the shape of the ex-Happy Days Scanias.

Thamesdown Transport 15 (A 95 FRY) was a Dennis Falcon with Duple Dominant bus body on loan to MRN for a few weeks in October 1988.

MRN took a DAF/Optare Delta demonstrator for a period in 1990. It is seen at Crown Bridge, Penkridge on a Stafford-Wolverhampton roster. No orders arose from this exercise.

South Yorkshire Transport loaned one of its Dennis Dominator/Alexander double-deckers to MRN in July 1988. 2483 is seen on return to Cannock garage at the end of its late duty.

Charles Roberts

Grimsby-Cleethorpes Transport 28 (E 938 PBE), a Leyland Tiger with dual-purpose Alexander P-type body, was on loan for some four weeks in 1989. It is seen at Stafford Station awaiting departure on route 825 to Tamworth.

All 'Tellus' Transits of the 1986 batch were sent on extended loan to Blackpool Transport during the summer of 1987, their place at Wellington being taken by Transits displaced from the Walsall venture. 42 is seen in suitable surroundings with the Blackpool Tower. Charles Roberts

COMPETITORS AND FRIENDS

Seen at Chester Interchange is fellow British Bus operator Crosville Wales' B Series Leyland National GMB 660 T (SNL 660); some of the same batch came to MRN.

One of Midland Red West's numerous Leyland Lynx buses prepares to leave Shrewsbury at the late afternoon rush hour for Ludlow.

Happy Days' 170 (G 612 CFA) was one of three Scania K93CRB/Plaxton buses purchased in 1990. These buses, together with a Ford Transit minibus and an Alexander bodied Mercedes-Benz 814D, were acquired along with the stage carriage interests of Happy Days in 1991. The scene is Newport High Street, Shropshire.

Frontline Buses Leyland Tiger YSU 953 shows off its Plaxton Paramount body to advantage in the red livery used by that operator. Note the badger at the rear.

GM Buses 2014, a Northern Counties bodied Leyland Olympian, had recently become one of the split GMB South fleet when seen in central Manchester in the summer of 1994.

One of the less attractive features of deregulation has been the competition from operators who are prepared to use elderly, and in some cases shabby, second-hand vehicles as a means of undercutting the operating costs of the established operators. An example of the syndrome is this anonymous Seddon Pennine 7 with Alexander AY body, ex-Western Scottish, at the Chester Interchange.

PMT's regular contribution to the X64 Hanley-Shrewsbury service is a Plaxton Paramount bodied Leyland Tiger. Here their STL24, dating from 1983, picks up for Shrewsbury at Market Drayton, with the MRN Hanley-bound coach standing astern.

Former Midland Red (and MRN) Leyland Leopard 207 (JHA 207 L) was snapped up, with others of BMMO type LS 27, by Chase Bus Services in 1987. It actually appeared soon afterwards on services deregistered by its former owners although here it is seen in Walsall on a 'Centro' tendered service.

Gordon Weston

Green Bus Service 19 (DUH 77 V) enters Queens Square, Wolverhampton. As is usual for this operator the bus is smartly turned out. It was new to Rhondda Transport.

One of Williamsons fleet, a 1979 Leyland Leopard/Plaxton coach, is seen parked at one of the peripheral stances at Shrewsbury bus station. These stances are used for the country services.

Stevensons were unusual in having eleven of the comparatively rare Leyland Swift in the fleet, Leyland's belated attempt to carve a niche in the developing midibus market. One of the breed, 66, is seen approaching Rugeley bus station. It has a Wadham Stringer 39-seat body and was one of five similar buses.

Of West Midlands numerous MCW Metrobuses 2268 was an earlier example, one of the large intake of 1980-1981. It is seen in Wolverhampton complete with the new style fleet name incorporating the garage designation. The small green circle on the windscreen also identifies the garage, in this case with the letters CR. This originally indicated Cleveland Road but with the closure of those premises for redevelopment Wolverhampton buses are now housed at another garage, returned to service from mothballed condition, at Park Lane.

Star Line of Knutsford operates a large fleet of Mercedes-Benz midibuses on its services in south Manchester and Cheshire. One of these, H 407 BVR, was observed at Macclesfield operating Star Line's 487 service to Wilmslow.

NEW EXISTENCES

Right: Midland Red 234, a type LS27 Marshall bodied Leyland Leopard, lives on in the territory where it served for so many years. It was purchased, with support from Barclays Bank, by Walton High School, Stafford, where it is seen in the autumn of 1994. There is concern that the likely impact of seat belt regulations may mean the end of the road for this excellent specimen and it is hoped that in some way preservation can become a possibility.

Below left: Leyland National 477 went with four others to London Country (South West) in 1987. Its new owners subsequently sent it to Blackburn where East Lancs converted it to a Greenway, in which form it is seen operating on a London Transport tendered service. This Ray Stenning livery was perhaps the most attractive of the Drawlane corporate style .   Charles Roberts

Below right: Leyland National GOL 433 N had been one of the earliest of the type in the Midland Red North fleet as its 433. It was one of eight which went to the North East in 1987 to become Northumbria 720.   Charles Roberts

ODDS AND ENDS

First bus stop design of the Drawlane/British Bus era.

Second bus stop design of the Drawlane/British Bus era.

Cannock-based 1910 (EEH 910 Y) in advertising livery for National Travelworld is seen on its way to Birmingham bus station passing the Council House in Colmore Row. From the lack of traffic in central Birmingham it must have been either a Sunday or a Bank Holiday.

Two of the casualties of the Stafford fire stand in the yard at Delta Way. On the left Leyland National 989, formerly 689, (TOF 689 S) looks to be merely badly singed whilst only the bonnet of NCME bodied Renault, 342 remains more or less intact. Both of these buses were scrapped as being beyond economical repair.
Gordon Weston

Coach-seated Leyland Olympian 1913 carried for a time a broadside advertisement for McDonald's (no relation of the author) with a Tamworth yellow/red liveried front.

When the first two Freight Rover Sherpa vehicles with Carlyle bodies arrived on loan it was mooted that these, 201 as shown, 202 and subsequent deliveries would have shared ownership with Freight Rover owning the chassis and MRN the bodies. The Company Secretary of the time put paid to that scheme, for obvious reasons.
Charles Roberts

Quite the most outrageous livery used by the pre-privatisation management was the so-called 'Tellus Street Machine' concoction seen as applied to long-suffering National 768 outside Charlton Street garage, Wellington. Workshop Manager John Davis must have needed sunglasses.
Charles Roberts

Interurban and rural services operated by Midland Red North, January 1995

Service number	Service	Route details
2/2A	OSWESTRY - CHIRK - RUABON - WREXHAM	Gobowen or Weston Rhyn
9, 99	WELLINGTON - TELFORD - IRONBRIDGE - BRIDGNORTH	
31	HANDSACRE - CANNOCK - WALSALL - BIRMINGHAM	Rugeley, Hednesford, Bloxwich
34	BROWNHILLS - BURNTWOOD - LICHFIELD	Ogley Hay, Chase Terrace
38	CREWE - CONGLETON - MACCLESFIELD	Sandbach
39	WELLINGTON - TELFORD - MUCH WENLOCK	Ironbridge
81, 82, 83, 84	SHREWSBURY - TELFORD - NEWPORT - EDGMOND	Atcham, Wellington, Donnington
110	TAMWORTH - SUTTON COLDFIELD - BIRMINGHAM	Mile Oak, Erdington
116	TAMWORTH - KINGSBURY - BIRMINGHAM	Dosthill, Minworth, Tyburn
156	CANNOCK - BROWNHILLS - BIRMINGHAM	Heath Hayes, Aldridge, Kingstanding
158	BLOXWICH - ALDRIDGE - BIRMINGHAM	Kingstanding
221, 222	WHITCHURCH - PREES - WEM	Tilstock, Higher Heath, Soulton
243	ELLESMERE - WREXHAM	Chirk
278	OSWESTRY - WHITTINGTON - ELLESMERE	
345	WALSALL - BROWNHILLS	Rushall
346	WALSALL - PELSALL - BLOXWICH	Rushall
357	WALSALL - ALDRIDGE	Rushall
377	WALSALL - STREETLY - NEW OSCOTT	Foley Arms
416	CANNOCK - DUDLEY - MERRY HILL CENTRE	Hednesford, Black Country Museum
429	OSWESTRY - WESTON LULLINGFIELDS	Eardiston
432	STAFFORD - ECCLESHALL - WOODSEAVES	Great Bridgford
433	ECCLESHALL - NEWPORT - WOLVERHAMPTON	Sherrifhales, Weston Park
434	STAFFORD - WHEATON ASTON	Church Eaton
436	STAFFORD - MARKET DRAYTON - TELFORD	Eccleshall, Edgmond, Newport
437	STAFFORD - SHEBDON	Eccleshall
439	STAFFORD - ECCLESHALL - MARKET DRAYTON	Bishops Offley, Cheswardine
449	OSWESTRY - WELSHAMPTON	Ellesmere
454, 455	OSWESTRY - LLANSILIN	Rhydycroesau, Croesau Bach
481	STAFFORD - NEWPORT - TELFORD - WELLINGTON	Gnosall, Donnington
492	STAFFORD - STONE - ECCLESHALL	Yarnfield
501	SHREWSBURY - ELLESMERE	Myddle
516, 517	WOLVERHAMPTON - COMPTON - PATTINGHAM	Wightwick
519	SHREWSBURY - HIGH ERCALL - NEWPORT	Roden, Crudgington, Edgmond
546	SHREWSBURY - PULVERBATCH	Longden
553	SHREWSBURY - PLOX GREEN	Minsterley, Pontesbury
575	SHREWSBURY - WESTON LULLINGFIELDS	Montford Bridge, Ruyton XI Towns
576	SHREWSBURY - BASCHURCH - OSWESTRY	Bomere Heath, Ruyton XI Towns
579	SHREWSBURY - WILCOTT	Bomere Heath, Montford
606	MERE GREEN - SUTTON COLDFIELD - ERDINGTON	Wylde Green
623	SUTTON COLDFIELD - MINWORTH	Walmley
766	TAMWORTH - ATHERSTONE	Fazeley, Wilnecote, Dordon
775	TAMWORTH - LICHFIELD	Hopwas, Whittington
785	TAMWORTH - SHUTTINGTON - WARTON	Amington , Austrey
786	TAMWORTH - POLESWORTH - AUSTREY	Birchmoor
788	TAMWORTH - DRAYTON BASSETT	Fazeley
823	STAFFORD - RUGELEY - LICHFIELD	Milford, Little Haywood, Colwich, Longdon
825	STAFFORD - RUGELEY - LICHFIELD - TAMWORTH	Milford, Little Haywood, Colwich, Handsacre
832	BURNTWOOD - HEDNESFORD - STAFFORD	Chase Terrace, Norton Canes, Pye Green
836	CANNOCK - STAFFORD	Huntington
838	CANNOCK - STAFFORD	Jubilee Inn, Huntington
841	STAFFORD - COLWICH - HIXON	Little Haywood
842	STAFFORD - WESTON - HIXON	
843	STAFFORD - PENKRIDGE	Bednall
860	CANNOCK - BURNTWOOD - LICHFIELD	Heath Hayes, Norton Canes
862	CANNOCK - BURNTWOOD - LICHFIELD	Hednesford, Rawnsley, Cannock Wood
870	CANNOCK - FEATHERSTONE - WOLVERHAMPTON	Cheslyn Hay
871	CANNOCK - FEATHERSTONE - WOLVERHAMPTON	Wedges Mills, Cheslyn Hay
872	CANNOCK - FEATHERSTONE - WOLVERHAMPTON	Wedges Mills
873	STAFFORD - PENKRIDGE - WOLVERHAMPTON	Gailey, Coven
876	STAFFORD - PENKRIDGE - WOLVERHAMPTON	Gailey, Coven, Brewood
890	WOLVERHAMPTON - BRIDGNORTH	Compton, Wightwick, Rudge Heath
891	WOLVERHAMPTON - TELFORD - WELLINGTON	Albrighton, Shifnal, Oakengates
C84	HANLEY - NEWCASTLE - CREWE - CHESTER	Madeley, Nantwich, Tarporley
D53, D63	OSWESTRY - ELLESMERE	Orthopaedic Hospital, Gobowen, Ifton Heath
D54	OSWESTRY - BRYN	Trefonen
D70	SHREWSBURY - OSWESTRY	A5, Montford Bridge, Whittington
D71	OSWESTRY - WELSHPOOL	Pant, Guilsfield
D75	SHREWSBURY-WELSHPOOL-NEWTOWN-LLANIDLOES	Caersws
K28	NANTWICH - LEIGHTON HOSPITAL	Wistaston
K29, K39	CREWE - AUDLEM / WALGHERTON	
K31	CREWE - WINSFORD - NORTHWICH	Leighton Hospital
K32	CREWE - SANDBACH COMMON	Coppenhall
K33, K37	CREWE - SANDBACH - WINSFORD	Middlewich
K34	CREWE - HASLINGTON	
K54	CREWE - OCCLESTONE	
X25	STAFFORD - LICHFIELD - TAMWORTH	Milford, Rugeley
X64	SHREWSBURY - MARKET DRAYTON - HANLEY	Newcastle - under - Lyme
X74	TAMWORTH - M42 - BIRMINGHAM	Stoneydelph, Tyburn House
X76	NUNEATON - TAMWORTH - BIRMINGHAM	Atherstone, Drayton Manor Park, Tyburn
X86	STAFFORD - PENKRIDGE - BIRMINGHAM	

Index

127